Dictionary
of
Babies Names

DICTIONARY

OF

BABIES NAMES

David Geddes

CAXTON REFERENCE

© 2001 Caxton Editions

This edition published 2001 by Caxton Publishing Group Ltd,
20 Bloomsbury Street, London, WC1B 3QA.

Design and compilation by The Partnership Publishing Solutions Ltd,
Glasgow, G77 5UN

Printed and bound in India

Introduction

If you are reading this introduction you are almost certainly at a very exciting time in your life. Whether you are already a parent who is still undecided, a parent to be, grandparent, uncle, aunt, cousin or just a good friend of the people expecting the baby, we hope this book will assist you in the search for an appropriate name for the new arrival. The name that is chosen will last for a lifetime, so offer advice and choose wisely!

There is much to consider when choosing a name. Ideally both parents should be happy with the name. A good way of gauging your partner's preferences is each list as many boy's and girl's names that you consider acceptable, with your favourites at the top. Then read out the list and see what names appear on both lists – this can be very interesting and may cause some laughter! It may also throw up new names which one of you has not considered, but like. Once you have done this, go through this book, page by page, and discuss further names that were not on your list. This process can lead nowhere at times, so then it is time for bartering! Maybe you will agree to select a girl's name and your partner a boy's name, compromise is now the name of the game. Perhaps you may chose to use one of your preferred names as a middle name, keeping you both happy.

Middle names should not be forgotten as they can at times appease friends and relatives while not committing to call your child a certain name, especially where they are very old fashioned or just unacceptable to you. This approach may be useful where there are traditional family names that you are unhappy with but are expected to use. Remember you can use more than one middle name although using eleven to call your child after your favourite football team is possibly extreme! In addition, when using middle names, consider the initials that your child will have as they may be teased by other children if their names give rise to BUG, SAD or STY for example.

Considering the point about the football team, you should be careful when choosing the name of a favourite movie, TV, sport or music star. These names tend to be popular for a short period of time and there are usually a lot of parents who name their children this way. Remember you will view the baby as an individual, so when a shout goes up in the playground it is best if your child doesn't answer with another ten or so pupils!

Names of family and friends can be helpful to us. Consider the names of people around you or those you have known in the past. Do you have a warmth or attraction to the name because of the person you think of? This could influence your decision greatly. Do you like your own name? Do you feel comfortable with it and feel it has served you well over the years? To have a baby named after you is a great honour indeed although you must be careful not to try and turn the child into a clone as each child has their own life to lead.

Derivatives of names should also be considered. If you call your son Michael, are you happy with Mike, Mick and Micky? Your daughter, Charlotte, can become Lottie, Charlie or Chattie. There is no doubt somebody will use a shortened form at some point in their life. In fact, it may be the child themself who adopts a derivative when they grow up, so be sure to chose carefully. Also, the relationship between the chosen first name and the baby's surname should be taken into account. Would you want your child to be known as Albert Hall, Trent River or Benedict Monk? Some people wouldn't care, however, consider how the child may feel in later life. Other tips which can help minimise confusion are to use a different initial letter from that of other family members, as in the future if there are more than one Mr B Smith in the family, mail may be opened by the wrong person. In addition, confusion can sometimes abound if the name can be used for both sexes, e.g. Lesley. These are of course only tips and should not be taken as golden rules, especially if in your opinion, the perfect name for the baby is Lesley in a family of Lionel, Laura and Luke Smith!

Dictionary of Babies Names

There is a comprehensive list of names in this book which were compiled from many sources. One major source of names that dates back for thousands of years is the bible. In the text you may note these listed as Hebrew. Some of these great names from the Old Testament convey a sense of authority and greatness that make them attractive to parents wishing the best for their child e.g. Joshua, Daniel, Samson and Noah. From the New Testament the names of the writers' of the gospels, Matthew, Mark, Luke and John are to this day widely used as are others from The New Testament e.g. Paul, Thomas and Stephen. These names are traditional yet timeless.

In this book there are also many names that have come to us from cultures and areas of the world near and far and we include Sanskrit, Greek, Old French, Latin and Old German names alongside Saxon, Irish, Scots and Welsh. These names have been introduced to our country down through the years as we have became a more multi-cultural society. The introduction of these influences has added colour and variety to the names we now choose. This has also meant that generally there is far more choice in naming your baby today, compared to our parents and grandparent's days. These very diverse influences should ensure fun and much comment when considering the name to be chosen. You may be surprised by the reaction of older friends and relatives who can be more adventurous with names that were not available to them, in fact, maybe your name would have been quite different if they could take this book back in time!

Of course, you may have already chosen the name for your baby. We hope that this book can help with the origin of the name and possibly detail derivatives that you may want to use as pet names. Pet names are very much part of our society, with many baring no relation to the baby's first name, however, you may find in this book a pet name you had not thought of or not realised was linked to a first name.

As mentioned in the opening paragraph, naming a baby is a very exciting task that brings with it many considerations and a great deal of responsibility. Take your time to find the correct name in order that it feels right for the baby concerned. We hope that you enjoy reading through and considering the names in this book and feel that your final choice is one which you are proud to pass on as the first of many precious gifts to the baby in question.

Aaron *m*
Probably an Egyptian name, but the meaning is unknown.
Aaron was the brother of Moses and first High Priest of Israel.

Abdullah *m*
Arabic in origin, meaning 'servant of Allah'. The shortened
form is Abdul.

Abel *m*
A Hebrew name, the meaning of which is doubtful. Abel was
the second son of Adam and Eve.

Abigail *f*
(Hebrew); meaning 'father's happiness'; short forms are
Abbie, Abby and Gail.

Abner *m*
From the Hebrew, meaning 'father of light'. In the Old
Testament, Abner was the cousin of King Saul and
commander of his army.

Abraham *m*
Hebrew in origin. The name of the patriarch was originally
Abram meaning 'high father' but was changed to Abraham
'father of many nations'. Short forms are Abe, Abie, Ham.

Absalom *m*
From the Hebrew, meaing 'father of peace'. In the Bible,
Absalom was the rebellious son of King David.

Acacia *f*
(Greek); the name of a plant.

Ada *f*
A short form of Adelaide and Adela.

Adah *f*
(Hebrew); meaning 'a decoration'; another form is Ada.

Adam *m*
From the Hebrew, meaning 'red', describing the colour of skin. In the top twenty of popular boys' names.

Adama *f*
(Hebrew); meaning 'red'; the feminine form of Adam.

Adar *f*
(Hebrew); meaning 'fire'.

Adela *f*
(Old German); meaning 'noble'; another form from the French is Adele and the short forms are Addie and Addy.

Adelaide *f*
(Old German); meaning 'high-born'; the short form is Ada.

Adeline *f*
(Old German); meaning 'noble'; the short forms are Alina and Aline.

Adelphia *f*
(Greek); meaning 'sisterly'.

Adil *m*
Arabic in origin, meaning 'honest'. Also Adeel.

Adina *f*
(Hebrew); meaning 'responsible'.

Adolpha *f*

(Old German); meaning 'noble wolf'.

Adolphus *m*
An Old German name meaning 'noble wolf'. Used by various German royal families in the 17th and 18th centuries, it was brought to England by the Hanovarians. Also Adolf and Adolph.

Adora *f*
(Latin); meaning 'cherished gift'.

Adorabella *f*
(Latin); meaning 'lovely gift'.

Adrian *m*
From the Latin, meaning 'of the Adriatic'. A Roman emperor and several popes have held this name. St Adrian was the first British martyr in the 4th century. Adrian is a version of Hadrian, the Roman Emperor who built the wall across the north of England.

Adrienne *f*
(Latin); meaning 'from Adria'; other forms are Adrianne and Adriana.

Afra *see* **Aphra.**

Agatha *f*
(Greek); meaning 'good'; the short forms are Aggie and Aggy.

Aglaia *f*
(Greek); meaning 'beautiful'.

Agnes *f*
(Greek); meaning 'pure'; the short forms are Aggie, Aggy and Nessie; another form is Annis.

Ahmed *m*
Arabic meaning 'praiseworthy'; one of the names of the

prophet Muhammad. Also spelt Ahmad.

Aidan *m*
An Old Irish name meaning 'small fire'. The anglicised form is Edan.

Aileen *see* **Eileen.**

Ailsa *f*
A name derived from Ailsa Craig, the rock off the Scottish west coast.

Aimée *f*
The French form of Amy.

Ainsley *f*
A place name and surname used as a first name.

Aisha *f*
(Arabic); meaning 'flourishing'; other forms are Aiesha, Ayisha and Ayesha.

Aisling *f*
(Irish); meaning 'a dream'; another form is Aisleen.

Aithne *f*
(Irish); meaning 'fire'; another form is Aine.

Ajay *m*
The Sanskrit name meaning 'invincible'.

Alan *m*
A Celtic name, the meaning of which is doubtful. The name of an early Welsh saint, it was introduced into England at the time of the Norman Conquest. Especially popular in Scotland. Other spellings are Allan, Allen, Alun, Alain (French).

Alana *f*

The feminine form of Alan; other forms are Alanna and Lana.

Alastair *m*
(Gaelic); defender of men; form of Alexander; also Alasdair, Alistair.

Albert *m*
(Old German); noble and bright; short forms are Bert and Al.

Alberta *f*
The feminine form of Albert.

Albina *f*
(Latin); meaning 'fair-haired'; another form is Albinia.

Alcina *f*
(Greek); meaning 'strong of mind'.

Alda *f*
(Old German); meaning 'old'.

Aldora *f*
(Old English); meaning 'high-born'.

Aldous *m*
(Old German); old; the form Aldo is used in North America.

Aldwyn *m*
(Anglo-Saxon); old friend; alternative spelling is Aldwin.

Alethea *f*
(Greek); meaning 'truth'.

Alexander *m*
(Greek); defender of men; there are many short forms – Al, Alec, Alex and Sandy. In the top twenty of popular boys' names.

Alexandra *f*
The feminine form of Alexander; other forms are Alexandria

and Alexandrina; Sandra was also a form but is now a separate name with short forms Sandie and Sandy.

Alexis *m* and *f*
(Greek); meaning 'helpmate' or defender; other feminine forms are Alexia and Alexa.

Alfred *m*
(Old English); good counsellor; short forms are Alf, Alfie and Fred.

Alfreda *f*
The feminine form of Alfred; other forms are Elfreda, Elfrida and Freda.

Algernon *m*
(Old French); whiskered; much used in the 19th century but not so popular today; short forms Algie and Algy.

Ali *m*
(Arabic); excellent or noble.

Ali *f*
A short form of Alice and Alison.

Alia *f*
(Old German); meaning 'all'.

Alice *f*
(Old German); meaning 'noble'; other forms are Alicia, Alyssa, Alysia and Ailish; the short forms are Ali, Allie and Alley.

Alida *f*
A central European form of Adelaide.

Alima *f*
(Arabic); meaning 'musical'.

Aline *f*
A short form of Adeline.

Alison *f*
This name was originally a short form of Alice and is now used as a separate name; other forms are Allison and Allyson and the short forms are Allie and Ally.

Alissa *see* **Alice.**

Allegra *f*
(Italian); meaning 'cheerful and full of life'.

Alma *f*
(Latin); meaning 'loving and kind'.

Almira *f*
(Arabic); meaning 'princess'.

Aloysius *m*
(Latin); an old form of Louis or Lewis.

Alta *f*
(Latin); meaning 'noble'.

Althea *f*
(Greek); meaning 'virtuous'; the short form is Thea.

Alura *f*
(Old English); meaning 'counsellor'.

Alvina *f*
(Old German); meaning 'dear friend'; the short form is Vina.

Alys, Alyssa *f*
Other forms of Alice.

Alyth *f*
A place name used as a first name.

Amabel *f*
(Latin); meaning 'endearing'; the short form is Mabel, which is now an independent name.

Amalia *see* Amelia.

Amanda *f*
(Latin); meaning 'fit to be loved'; the short forms are Manda and Mandy.

Amaryllis *f*
(Greek); meaning possibly 'bright'.

Amber *f*
The name of the gemstone used as a first name.

Ambrin *f*
(Arabic); meaning 'ambergris', a sweet substance used in the manufacture of perfume; another form is Ambreen.

Ambrose *m*
(Greek); pertaining to the immortals.

Ambrosine *f*
The feminine form of Ambrose.

Amelia *f*
(Old German); meaning 'labour'; other forms are Amalia, Amalie and Amalita and the short form is Milly.

Amethyst *f*
The name of the gemstone used as a first name.

Amin *m*
(Arabic); trustworthy.

Amina *f*
(Arabic); meaning 'honest'; other forms are Amena and Aamena.

Aminta *f*
(Greek); meaning 'protector'; another form is Amynta and the short forms are Minta and Minty.

Amit *m*
(Sanskrit); without limit.

Amos *m*
(Hebrew); bearer of a burden.

Amrita *f*
(Sanskrit); meaning 'water of life'.

Amy *f*
(Old French); meaning 'beloved'; the French form is Aimée and other forms are Amata and Aimie. In the top twenty of popular girls' names.

Anais *f*
(Greek); meaning 'plentiful'.

Anand *m*
(Sanskrit); happiness or joy.

Ananda *f*
(Sanskrit); meaning 'happiness'; other forms are Anandi and Anandamayi.

Anastasia *f*
(Greek); meaning 'resurrection'; short forms are Nastasia, Stacey and Stacy.

Ancilla *f*
(Latin); meaning 'a handmaid'.

Andrea *f*
The feminine form of Andrew; other forms are Andrée, Andrene, Andrena and Andrina.

Andrew *m*
(Greek); manly; the name of the patron saint of Scotland; short forms are Andy, Drew and André (French).

Aneka *see* Anne.

Aneurin *m*
(Welsh); noble, honourable; short form Nye.

Angela *f*
(Greek); meaning 'a messenger'; other forms are Angel, Angelique, Angelica and Angeline and the short form is Angie.

Angelica *f*
(Latin); meaning 'angelic'.

Angharad *f*
(Welsh); meaning 'well loved'.

Angus *m*
(Gaelic); one choice; this is a popular Scottish name. The Irish form is Aonghus

Anila *f*
(Sanskrit); meaning 'air'.

Ann *f*
(Hebrew); meaning 'favoured by God'; this name is derived from Hannah and other forms are Anne, Anna, Anita, Annette and Anona; the short forms are Nan, Nanette, Nancy and Annie; the Dutch form is Aneka or Anneka.

Annabel *f*
The meaning is uncertain and it was used originally in Scotland; other forms are Annabelle and Annabella and the short forms are Bella and Belle.

Annan *m*

(Gaelic); water; a Scottish place name used as a first name.

Annis *see* **Agnes.**

Anona *f*
May be the Welsh form of Ann; another form is Annona and the short form is Nona.

Anora *f*
(Latin); meaning 'beauty'; another form is Annora.

Anthea *f*
(Greek); meaning 'flowery'.

Anthony *m*
(Latin); the meaning is unknown; another form is Antony and short form is Tony.

Antonia *f*
The feminine form of Antony; another form is Antoinette and the short forms are Toni, Tonya, Net and Nettie.

Anwen *f*
(Welsh); meaning 'beautiful'.

Aonghas *m*
(Irish); the Irish form of Angus.

Aphra *f*
(Hebrew); meaning 'dust'; another form is Afra.

April *f*
The name of the month used as a first name.

Arabella *f*
(Latin); the meaning is uncertain but may be 'obliging'; other forms are Arabel and Arabelle and the short forms are Bel, Belle and Bella.

Araminta *f*

(Greek): meaning 'protector'; the short forms are Minta and Minty.

Archibald *m*
(Old German); genuinely bold; short form Archie.

Aretha *f*
(Greek); meaning 'virtue'; other forms are Areta and Aretta.

Argenta *f*
(Latin); meaning 'silver'.

Aria *f*
(Italian); meaning 'air' or 'a song'.

Ariadne *f*
(Greek); meaning 'very holy'; the French form is Arianne and the Italian is Arianna.

Ariel *f*
The meaning is uncertain; other forms are Arial and Arielle.

Arjun *m*
(Sanskrit); bright.

Arlene *f*
This a modern name and other forms are Arleen and Arline.

Arminel *f*
This is a rare name which could be a short form of Armine.

Arnold *m*
(Old German); power of an eagle; short form Arnie.

Artemisia *f*
(Greek); meaning 'belonging to Artemis', the Greek goddess of the moon and hunting.

Arthur *m*
(Celtic); a bear; the original popularity of this name came

from the association with King Arthur; short forms Art or Arty; the Italian and Spanish form is Arturo.

Arun *m*
(Sanskrit); reddish brown.

Aruna *f*
(Sanskrit); meaning 'reddish brown'; another form is Arumina.

Asa *m*
(Hebrew); physician.

Asha *f*
(Sanskrit); meaning 'hope and desire'.

Ashley *m* and *f*
(Old English); meaning ash field; short form Ash.

Ashraf *m*
(Arabic); more noble; a much used Muslim name.

Aslam *m*
(Arabic); safer.

Asma *f*
(Arabic); meaning 'eminent and powerful'.

Aspasia *f*
(Greek); meaning 'welcome'.

Astrid *f*
(Old Norse); meaning 'strong god'.

Atalanta *f*
The name of a beautiful girl in Greek mythology who said that she would only marry a man who could run faster than herself.

Athene *f*

Athol

The name of a Greek goddess; another form is Athena.

Athol *m* and *f*
(Gaelic); meaning New Ireland; a Scottish place name and surname used as a first name; another form is Atholl.

Aubrey *m*
(Old German); spirit ruler; related names are Auberon and Oberon.

Audrey *f*
(Old English); meaning 'noble strength'.

Augusta *f*
(Latin); meaning 'reverenced'; another form is Augustina and the short forms are Gus and Gussie.

Augustus *m*
(Latin); venerable or consecrated; other form Austin; short form Gus.

Aurea *f*
(Latin); meaning 'golden'.

Aurelia *f*
(Latin); meaning 'golden'; other forms are Auriel, Oriel and Oriole.

Aurora *f*
The name of the goddess of the dawn.

Ava *f*
A modern name whose origin is unknown.

Aveline *see* **Evelyn.**

Averil *f*
(Old English); the meaning is uncertain; another form is Averill.

Avis *f*
This is a rare name and the meaning is uncertain.

Avril *f*
The French form of April.

Aylmer *m*
(Old English); noble and famous; the American form is
Elmer.

Aylwin *m*
(Old English); noble friend; other form is Alwin.

Azariah *m*
(Hebrew); helped by Jehovah.

Azim *m*
(Arabic); determined.

Azima *f*
(Arabic); meaning 'tenacious'.

Azure *f*
(French); meaning 'blue'; another form is Azura.

B

Babette *see* **Barbara and Elizabeth.**

Babs *see* **Barbara.**

Baird *m*
(Celtic); minstrel; a Scottish surname used as a first name.

Bala *f*
(Sanskrit); meaning 'a young child'.

Baldric *m*
(Old German); bold rule; other form Baudric.

Baldwin *m*
(Old German); bold friend.

Barbara *f*
(Greek); meaning 'foreign' or 'strange'; another form is Barbra
and the French form is Babette; the short forms are Bab,
Babs, Barbie and Bobbi.

Barnaby *m*
(Hebrew); son of consolation; this is a short form of
Barnabas; short form Barney.

Barry *m*
(Irish); spear; other form Barrie.

Bartholomew *m*
(Hebrew); son of Talmai; short forms are Bart, Barty and Bat.

Basil *m*
(Greek); kingly; the name has been used since the times of the Crusades.

Basilia *f*
The feminine form of Basil; another form is Basilie.

Bathsheba *f*
(Hebrew); meaning 'daughter of prosperity'; the short form is Sheba.

Beata *f*
(Latin); meaning 'blessed'; a short form is Bea.

Beatrice *f*
(Latin); meaning 'bearer of joy'; another form is Beatrix and the short forms are Bea, Beatie, Beatty, Trix and Trixie.

Becky *f*
A short form of Rebecca; another spelling is Beckie.

Bedelia *f*
This rather obscure name is used in Ireland and America.

Belinda *f*
This name comes from Old German but the meaning is uncertain; a short form is Bel.

Belle *f*
A short form of Annabel, Arabella and Isabel; another form is Bella.

Benedict *m*
(Latin); blessed; other forms Bennet and Benedick.

Benedicta *f*
(Latin); meaning 'blessed'.

Benjamin *m*

(Hebrew); son of the south; short forms are Ben, Benny and Bennie. In the top twenty of popular boys' names.

Berenice *f*
(Greek); meaning 'bringer of victory'; another form is Bernice and a short form is Bunny.

Bernadette *f*
The feminine form of Bernard; another form is Bernadine and the short form is Bernie; the Italian version is Bernadetta.

Bernard *m*
(Old German); brave bear; short forms are Bernie and Barney.

Bertha *f*
(Old English); meaning 'bright'; another form is Berta.

Bertram *m*
(Old German); bright raven; the French form is Bertrand and the short forms are Bert and Bertie.

Beryl *f*
(Greek); the name of a precious stone.

Bess, Bessie *see* Elizabeth.

Beth *f*
A short form of Elizabeth which is now a name in its own right.

Bethany *f*
The village where Lazarus lived; the short form is Bethan. In the top twenty of popular girls' names.

Bethia *f*
(Hebrew); meaning 'worshipper of God'; another form is Betha.

Bettina *f*

Betty

An Italian form of Elizabeth.

Betty *see* **Elizabeth.**

Beulah *f*
(Hebrew); meaning 'married'.

Beverley *f*
A surname used as a first name; the short form is Bev.

Bharat *m*
(Sanskrit); being maintained; this is the Hindu name for India.

Bharati *f*
The name of the Hindu goddess of learning.

Bhaskar *m*
(Sanskrit); the sun.

Bhavini *f*
The name of the Hindu goddess Parvati.

Bhavna *f*
(Sanskrit); meaning 'wish'; another form is Bhavana.

Bianca *f*
The Italian form of Blanche now used as a separate name.

Biddy *see* **Bridget.**

Billie *f*
This short form of the boy's name William is now being used as a girl's name.

Björn *m*
(Old Norse); bear.

Blaise *m*
(French); from the Blois region; other forms Blase or Blaze.

Blake *m*

(Old English); dark-complexioned; this is a first name derived from a surname.

Blair *m*

(Gaelic); a plain; a surname and also a place name used as a first name.

Blanche *f*

(French); meaning 'white'.

Blodwen *f*

(Welsh); meaning 'white flower'.

Blossom *f*

The English form of the French name Fleur.

Bobbie *f*

This short form of Roberta is now used as a separate name.

Bonamy *m*

(French); good friend.

Boniface *m*

(Latin); doer of good.

Bonny *f*

The Scottish word for 'pretty'; another form is Bonnie.

Boris *m*

(Russian); fight; one of the more popular Russian names in the 20th century.

Boyd *m*

(Gaelic); yellow-haired.

Bradley *m*

(Old English); broad meadow; the short form is Brad.

Brenda *f*

Brendan

(Old Norse); meaning 'a sword'; this name is also a feminine form of Brendan.

Brendan *m*
(Irish); meaning either 'stinking hair' or 'prince'; other forms are Brandon, Brandin or Brenden.

Brenna *f*
The feminine form of Brennan.

Bret *m*
(Old French); a Breton; another form is Brett.

Brian *m*
(Celtic); strong; other forms are Bryan, Brien and Brion.

Brianna *f*
The feminine form of Brian; other forms are Brianne and Bryony.

Brice *m*
(Celtic); of unknown meaning; another form is Bryce.

Bridget *f*
(Irish); the name of a Celtic fire goddess; other forms are Brigid and Bride and the short forms are Biddy and Bridie.

Brigham *m*
(Old English); meaning 'homestead by a bridge'; a surname used as a first name.

Brigitte *f*
The French form of Bridget.

Britt *f*
A short form of the Swedish Birgit which is now a name in its own right.

Brittany *f*

A name derived from the French region of Bretagne.

Broderick *m*
(Gaelic); brother; a surname used as a first name.

Bronwen *f*
(Welsh); meaning 'white breast'; another form is Bronwyn.

Brook *m* and *f*
A surname used as a first name; other forms are Brooke and Brooks.

Bruce *m*
(Old French); the meaning is unknown; the surname of a family which moved to Britain and especially Scotland after the Norman Conquest. A descendent was Robert the Bruce, King of Scots.

Bruno *m*
(German); brown; a German first name now used in Britain and America.

Bryn *m*
(Welsh); a hill; other forms are Brin and Brynmor.

Bryony *f*
The name of a plant used as a girl's name; another form is Briony.

Buck *m*
(Old English); stag or dashing young man; usually used as a nickname.

Buddy *m*
(Old English); friend or brother; normally used as a nickname.

Bunny *see* **Berenice.**

Bunty

Bunty *f*
A name for a pet lamb which is also used as a nickname.

Burhan *m*
(Arabic); proof; evidence.

Burl *m*
(Old English); bearer of the cup.

Burn *m*
(Old English); stream, brook; a surname used as a first name; other forms are Burne, Bourn, Bourne and Byrne.

Burton *m*
(Old English); a fortified farmstead; a surname used as a first name; the short form of Burt is now used independently.

Byron *m*
(Old English); a barn; although this name recalls Lord Byron, it is more often used in America.

C

Caddy *f*
A short form of Caroline, Carole and Carolyn.

Cadell *m*
(Welsh); battle spirit; a surname used as a first name.

Cadence *f*
(Latin); meaning 'rhythm'.

Cadfael *m*
(Welsh); battle metal.

Cadmus *m*
(Greek); man from the east.

Cadwallader *m*
(Welsh); battle leader.

Cain *m*
(Hebrew); possession; the son of Adam and Eve who killed his younger brother Abel.

Caitlin *f*
An Irish form of Katherine.

Caleb *m*
(Hebrew); intrepid; popular in America; short form Cale.

Caley *m*
(Irish); slender; the short form of Calum.

Calhoun *m*
(Irish); from the forest; a surname used as a first name.

Callie *f*
A short form of Caroline, and some other names, which is now used separately; other forms are Cally and Cal.

Callum *m*
(Latin); a dove; a name related to Malcolm; other forms are Calum, Cally and Caley. In the top twenty of popular boys' names.

Calvin *m*
Old French); bald; short form is Cal.

Cameron *m*
(Gaelic); crooked nose; a surname used as a first name.

Camilla *f*
The name of a warrior queen from Roman legend; the French form is Camille and the short forms are Milly and Millie.

Campbell *m*
(Gaelic); crooked mouth; a surname used as a first name.

Candace *f*
A name used by the queens of Ethiopia; another form is Candice and the short forms are Candy and Candie.

Candida *f*
(Latin); meaning 'white'.

Canute *m*
(Old Norse); a knot; the name of an early English King; short forms Cnut and Knut.

Cara *f*
(Italian); meaning 'darling'; another form is Kara and other names derived from Cara are Carissa and Carina.

Caradoc *m*
(Welsh); beloved.

Carey *m*
Welsh); dweller in a castle.

Carl *m*
(German); strong, noble; a German form of Charles; other form Karl.

Carla *f*
The feminine form of Carl; other forms are Karla, Carlie and Carly.

Carlo *m*
The Italian form of Charles.

Carlos *m*
The Spanish form of Charles.

Carlotta *f*
The Italian form of Charlotte.

Carlton *m*
(Old English); the peasant's farm; a place name and a surname used as a first name; other form Charlton.

Carmel *f*
(Hebrew); meaning 'a garden'; the Spanish form is Carmen and Carmela the Italian; the short forms are Carmelita and Carmelina.

Carmichael *m*
(Celtic); Michael's fort; a place name and a surname used as a first name.

Carnation *f*
The name of a flower used as a first name.

Carol *m*
(Latin); strong, noble; derived from the latinized form of Charles; also Karol or Karel.

Carol *f*
This was originally a short form of Caroline; other forms are Carole and Carola; the short forms are Caro, Caddie and Caddy.

Caroline *f*
This name was originally the Italian form of Charles; other forms are Carolyn and Carolina; short forms are Carrie, Caro and Lyn.

Carr *m*
(Old Norse); an overgrown marsh; a place name and a surname used as a first name.

Carrick *m*
(Gaelic); a rock; a place name used as a first name.

Carter *m*
(Old English); a driver or maker of carts; a surname used as a first name.

Carver *m*
(Cornish); a great rock; a surname used as a first name.

Carwyn *m*
(Welsh); blessed love.

Cary *m*
(Irish); dark brown; a surname used as a first name; another form is Carey.

Casey *m* and *f*
(Irish); vigilant in war; a surname used as a first name; also a form of the Polish name Casimir.

Cashel *m*

(Irish); a stone fort; a place name used as a first name.

Caspar *m*

The name of one of the wise men in the Christmas story; the English version is Jasper and other forms are Gasper and Gaspard (French).

Cassandra *f*

The name of a Greek prophetess whose prophesies were never believed; the short forms are Cass and Cassie.

Cassius *m*

(Latin); meaning 'empty'; another form is Cassian and the short form is Cass.

Cassidy *m* and *f*

(Irish); clever; a surname used as a first name; the short form is Cass.

Cathal *m*

(Irish); war leader.

Catherine *f*

Another form of Katherine; other forms are Catharine, Catherina and Catharina; the short forms are Cath, Cathie and Cathy.

Cato *m*

(Latin); wise one; a Roman surname used as a first name.

Catriona *f*

The Gaelic form of Katherine; other forms are Catrina and Katrina and the Welsh form is Catrin.

Cavan *m*

(Irish); meaning grassy hill; a place name used as a first name.

Cecil *m*
(Latin); blind; an aristocratic surname which became used as a first name.

Cecilia *f*
The feminine form of Cecil; other forms are Cecily, Cicely and Sisley and the French version is Cecile; the short forms are Celia, Sis, Ciss and Cissy.

Cedric *m*
A character in Sir Walter Scott's novel Ivanhoe; probably from Cerdic, king of Wessex.

Ceinwen *m*
(Welsh); blessed, beautiful.

Celeste *f*
(Latin); meaning 'heavenly'; other forms are Celestine and Celesta.

Cephas *m*
(Aramaic); a stone.

Ceri *f*
(Welsh); meaning 'love'; other forms are Cerian and Cerys.

Ceridwen *f*
(Welsh); meaning 'poetry' and 'white'.

Chad *m*
The meaning is unknown; the name is now quite popular in America.

Chaim *m*
Another form of Hyam.

Chandan *m*
(Sanskrit); sandlewood; this is a divine name in Hindu texts.

Chander *m*
(Sanskrit); the moon.

Chandler *m*
(Old French); seller of candles; a surname used as a first name.

Chandra *f*
(Sanskrit); meaning 'the moon'.

Chandrakala *f*
(Sanskrit); meaning 'moonbeams'.

Chandrakant *m*
(Sanskrit); loved by the moon.

Chandrakanta *f*
(Sanskrit); meaning 'moon beloved'.

Chanel *f*
The name of a French perfume which is now being used as a first name.

Chantal *f*
This is a modern French name which has become popular, especially in America; other forms are Chantel and Chantalle.

Chapman *m*
Old English); a merchant; a surname used as a first name.

Charis *f*
(Greek); meaning 'grace'.

Charity *f*
(Latin); meaning 'love'; the short form is Cherry.

Charlene *f*
A feminine form of Charles; other forms are Charleen and Sharlene.

Charles *m*
(Old German); manly, strong; short forms are Charlie, Chas, Chuck, Chae or Chay.

Charlotte *f*
This is another feminine form of Charles; the short forms are Lottie, Charlie and Chattie. In the top twenty of popular girls' names.

Charlton *see* Carlton.

Charmaine *f*
This is a modern name whose origins are uncertain; other forms are Charmian and Sharmaine.

Charulata *f*
An Indian name meaning 'lovely'.

Chase *m*
(Old French); a hunter; a surname used as a first name.

Chauncey *m*
(Old French); a chancellor; a surname used as a first name; other forms are Chaunce, Chance and Chancey.

Chelsea *f*
A modern name derived from an area in London.

Cherie *f*
(French); meaning 'darling'; other forms are Sherry, Sheree and Cher.

Cherry *see* Charity.

Cheryl *f*
Another form of Cherry and other versions are Sheril, Sheryl and Cher.

Chester *m*

(Old English); a fortified camp; a place name used as a first name.

Chetan *m*
(Indian); meaning 'awareness'.

Chiara *f*
The Italian form of Clara.

Chilton *m*
(Old English); a farm for children; a place name and surname used as a first name.

Chintana *f*
(Sanskrit); meaning 'contemplation'.

Chloe *f*
(Greek); meaning 'a green young shoot'. In the top ten of popular girls' names.

Chloris *f*
(Greek); meaning 'blooming'; another form is Cloris.

Chris *m*
A short form of Christopher.

Chrissie *see* **Christine.**

Christabel *f*
(Latin); meaning possibly a mixture of 'Christ' and 'beautiful'; another form is Christobel and the short forms are Chris, Chrissie and Chrissy.

Christian *m* and *f*
(Latin); a follower of Christ; short forms are Christie and Christy.

Christine *f*
Meaning 'a Christian'; other forms are Christen, Christiana

and Christina, the short forms are Chris and Chrissie.

Christmas *see* **Noel.**

Christoph *m*
The German form of Christopher.

Christopher *m*
(Greek); meaning 'bearing Christ'; St. Christopher is the patron saint of travellers; short forms are Chris, Christie and Kit.

Chuck *see* **Charles.**

Cian *m*
(Irish); ancient; English forms are Kean and Keane.

Ciaran *m*
(Irish); little and black; the English form is Kieran.

Cicely *f*
Another form of Cecilia.

Cilla *f*
A short form of Priscilla.

Cindy *f*
A short form of Cynthia and Lucinda; now often used as a separate name.

Clare *f*
(Latin); meaning 'clear'; the Latin form is Clara and other forms are Claire, Clarrie, Clarabel and Clarinda.

Clarence *m*
This name comes from the Duke of Clarence, son of Edward III of England.

Clarimond *f*
(Old English); meaning 'clear protection'.

Clarinda *see* **Clare.**

Clarissa *f*
(Latin); meaning 'brightest'; another form is Clarice and the short form is Clarrie.

Clark *m*
(Old French); a clerk; another form is Clarke.

Claud *m*
(Latin); lame; this name is derived from the Roman name Claudius; other forms are Claude (French) and Claudio (Italian and Spanish).

Claudia *f*
(Latin); meaning 'lame'; the French form is Claude, with the short forms Claudette and Claudine.

Claus *m*
Is a form of Klaus and is derived from Nicholas.

Clayton *m*
(Old English); a dwelling in clay; a place name and a surname used as a first name; the short form is Clay.

Clematis *f*
The name of a plant used as a first name.

Clemence *f*
(Latin); meaning 'gentleness'; another form is Clemency and the short forms are Clem and Clemmie.

Clement *m*
(Latin); mild and merciful; the short forms are Clem and Clemmie.

Clementine *f*
(Latin); meaning 'gentle'; another form is Clementina and the short forms are Clem and Clemmie.

Cleo *f*
(Greek); meaning 'fame of her father'; a short form of
Cleopatra.

Cleveland *m*
(Old English); hilly; a place name used as a first name.

Clifford *m*
(Old English); ford by the cliff; a surname used as a first
name; the short form is Cliff.

Clifton *m*
(Old English); meaning 'on a cliff'; a place name used as a
first name.

Clint *m*
A short form of Clinton which is now used separately as a
first name.

Clinton *m*
A place name and a surname which is now used as a first
name.

Cliona *f*
The name of a girl in Irish legend; other forms are Clidna and
Cliodna.

Clive *m*
(Old English); one who lives by the cliff; a surname used as a
first name.

Clodagh *f*
The name of an Irish river used as a first name.

Clorinda *f*
Another form of Clarinda.

Clotilda *f*
(Old German); meaning 'the noise of battle'; another form is

Clotilde.

Clover *f*
The name of a plant used as a first name.

Clovis *m*
(Old German); a warrior.

Clyde *m*
An ancient name for a Scottish river which became a surname and latterly a first name.

Cody *m* and *f*
(Irish); a helpful person; a surname used as a first name and particularly popular in America. Another form is Codie.

Col *m*
A short form of Colman.

Colby *m*
A place name and a surname now used as a first name, especially in America.

Coleman *m*
(Old English); swarthy man; a surname used as a first name; the short form is Cole.

Colette *f*
This is a French short form of Nicola which is now used as a separate name.

Colin *m*
This name is a short form of Nicholas and has been used independently for a long time.

Colleen *f*
(Irish); meaning 'a girl'.

Collier *m*

Colm

(Old English); a charcoal burner; a surname used as a first name; other forms are Colyer and Collyer.

Colm _m_
(Irish); a dove.

Colman _m_
(Irish); keeper of doves; short forms are Col and Cole.

Columbine _f_
The name of a plant used as a first name.

Conan _m_
(Irish); hound or wolf; a short form is Con.

Conn _m_
(Irish); wisdom.

Connall _m_
(Irish); a brave man.

Conor _m_
(Irish); meaning 'lover of dogs'; other forms are Connor and Con. In the top twenty of popular boys' names.

Conrad _m_
(Old German); bold counsellor; the short forms are Con, Curt and Kurt.

Conroy _m_
(Gaelic); wise.

Constance _f_
(Latin); meaning 'constancy'; other forms are Constantia, Constancy and Constantina; the short form is Connie.

Constant _m_
(Latin); faithful.

Constantine _m_

(Latin); constant, firm; the name of the first Christian Emperor of Rome.

Conway *m*
(Irish); of unknown meaning, a surname used as a first name.

Cooper *m*
(Old English); a barrel maker; a surname used as a first name.

Cora *f*
(Greek); meaning 'a girl'; another form is Corinna and the French form is Corinne.

Coral *f*
The name of the material from the sea used as a first name; the French form is Coralie.

Corbett *m*
(Old French); black-haired; a surname used as a first name; also Corbet.

Corbin *m*
(Old French); a raven; a surname used as a first name.

Cordelia *f*
(Latin); meaning 'heart'.

Corooran *m*
(Irish); meaning 'red-faced'; a surname used as a first name.

Corey *m* and *f*
(Irish); the meaning is unknown; a surname used as a first name; another m form is Cory, f forms are Cori and Corrie.

Corisande *f*
This is a name from medieval romance; the meaning is unknown.

Cormac *m*
(Irish); a charioteer; other forms are Cormack and Cormick.

Cornelia *f*
This is the feminine form of Cornelius, the surname of a Roman family.

Cornelius *m*
(Latin); a horn; this was a Roman family name; another form is Cornell.

Corwin *m*
(Old French); dear friend.

Cosima *f*
(Greek); meaning 'order'; this is the feminine form of Cosmo.

Cosmo *m*
(Greek); meaning 'order'; the Italian form is Cosimo.

Courtney *m*
(Old French); probably from 'court nez', short nose; a surname used as a first name.

Courtney *f*
A surname used as a first name; another form is Courtnay. In the top twenty of popular girls' names.

Craig *m*
(Gaelic); a crag.

Cranley *m*
(Old English); spring or meadow; a surname used as a first name.

Crawford *m*
(Old English); ford of the crows; a place name and a surname used as a first name.

Creighton *m*
(Old English); a rock; a surname used as a first name.

Cressida *f*
This is a name from ancient literature; the short form is Cressy.

Crispin *m*
(Latin); curled hair; another form is Crispian.

Cromwell *m*
A place name and a surname used as a first name.

Crosby *m*
(Old Norse); village or farm; a place name and surname used as a first name.

Crystal *f*
The name of a fine glass used as a first name; other forms are Cristal and Krystal.

Cullen *m*
(Gaelic); beyond the river; a place name used as a first name.

Culley *m*
(Gaelic); woodland; a surname used as a first name.

Curran *m*
(Irish); meaning unknown; a surname used as a first name.

Curtis *m*
(Old French); meaning courteous; a surname used as a first name.

Cuthbert *m*
(Old English); bright and famous.

Cynan *m*
(Welsh); outstanding; other forms are Cynin and Cynon.

Cynthia *f*

This name is one of the titles of the Greek goddess Artemis; the short forms are Cindy, Cindie and Cindi.

Cyril *m*

(Greek); lord; the short form is Cy.

Cyrus *m*

(Persian); meaning 'the sun'; the short forms are Cy and Cyro.

D

Daffodil *f*
The name of the flower used as a first name; the short form is Daffy.

Dafydd *m*
The Welsh form of David.

Dag *m*
(Old Norse); meaning 'day'.

Dagmar *f*
(Old Norse); meaning 'clear day'.

Dahlia *f*
The name of a plant used as a first name.

Dai *m*
(Welsh); shining; this name is also the Welsh diminutive form of David.

Daisy *f*
The name of the flower used as a first name; it was also a short form of Margaret.

Dakota *f*
The name of an American Indian nation used as a first name, especially in the USA.

Dale *m* and *f*
(Old English); a valley; a surname used as a first name.

Daley *m* and *f*
(Irish); a meeting; a surname used as a first name; another
form is Daly.

Dallas *m*
(Gaelic); a resting place; a surname used as a first name.

Dalton *m*
(Old English); a farm in the valley; a surname used as a first
name.

Damaris *f*
The name of an Athenian woman who was converted to
Christianity by St Paul.

Damian *m*
(Greek); meaning 'a tamer'.

Damon *m*
(Greek); a guide.

Dan *m*
A short form of Daniel.

Dana *m* and *f*
(Old English); meaning a Dane; a surname used as a first
name.

Danby *m*
(Old Norse); settlement of the Danes; a place name and a
surname used as a first name; a short form is Dan.

Dandie *m*
A Scottish short form of Andrew.

Daniel *m*
(Hebrew); 'God has judged'; Daniel was one of the Old
Testament prophets; short forms are Dan and Danny. In the
top ten of popular boys' names.

Danielle *f*
The feminine form of Daniel; other forms are Daniella and Danette.

Daphne *f*
(Greek); meaning 'laurel'.

Darcy *m*
(Old French); a man from Arcy; a surname used as a first name; another form is D'Arcy.

Darcy *f*
A surname used as a first name; other forms are Darcie and Darcey.

Daria *f*
The feminine form of Darius.

Darius *m*
(Persian); meaning 'protector'.

Darlene *f*
This is a modern name combining 'darling' with a suffix; another form is Darleen.

Darnell *m*
(Old English); hidden corner; a surname used as a first name.

Darrel *m*
(French); this was a surname which came from a French village and is now used as a first name; other forms are Darrell, Darell, Darryl and Daryl.

Darrell *f*
A surname used as a first name; other forms are Darrelle, Daryl and Darryl.

Darren *m*
This is a surname, meaning unknown, now used as a first

name.

Darshan *m*

(Sanskrit); meaning 'to see'; this is an Indian name.

David *m*

(Hebrew); meaning 'beloved'; David is the patron saint of Wales; short forms are Dave, Davie, and Davy; in Wales the name is Dafydd with short forms Dai and Taffy.

Davina *f*

This is the feminine form of David; another form is Davida and short forms are Vida and Vina.

Dawn *f*

This is a modern name although Aurora, the name of the Greek goddess of the dawn, was used earlier.

Dean *m*

(Old English); a valley; a surname used as a first name.

Dearborn *m*

(Old English); meaning 'brook of the deer'; a surname used as a first name.

Declan *m*

(Irish); this is the name of an early Irish saint which has now become popular in Ireland.

Deborah *f*

(Hebrew); meaning 'a bee'; a modern form is Debra and the short forms are Debbie and Debby.

Decima *f*

(Latin); meaning 'tenth'.

Dee *m* and *f*

This is usually a nickname but it is sometimes used as a first name. Deedee *f* is also used.

Deepak *m*

(Sanskrit); little lamp; another form is Dipak.

Deepika *f*

(Sanskrit); meaning 'little lamp'.

Deinol *m*

(Welsh); charming.

Deirdre *f*

(Irish); possibly meaning 'full of sorrow'.

Delbert *m*

This is a name which has come into use during this century; short forms are Del or Dell, which can also be familiar forms of Derek.

Delia *f*

A name given to Artemis, the Greek goddess of the moon.

Delilah *f*

(Hebrew); meaning 'a flirt'; the name of the woman who betrayed Samson; another form is Dalila and the short form is Lila.

Della *f*

This is a short form of Adela which is now a separate name.

Delmar *m*

(Latin); of the sea.

Delphine *f*

(Latin); meaning 'a dolphin'.

Demelza *f*

A place name used as a first name.

Demetrius *m*

(Greek); follower of the goddess of agriculture; other forms are Demitrus, Dimitri, and Dmitri.

Dempsey *m*
(Gaelic); proud descendent; a surname used as a first name.

Denis *m*
(Greek); this name comes from Dionysos, the Greek god of wine; another form is Dennis and short forms are Den and Denny.

Denise *f*
The feminine form of Denis; other forms are Dionne and Dione.

Dennison *m*
(Old English); the son of Dennis; another form is Denison.

Denton *m*
(Old English); a valley; a surname used as a first name.

Denver *m*
(Old English); the crossing of the Danes; a surname used as a first name.

Denzil *m*
(Celtic); meaning 'stronghold'; derived from a place name in Cornwall; other forms are Denzel and Denzell.

Derek *m*
(Old German); ruler of the people; this is now a popular name and other forms are Deryk, Deric and Dirk, which is the Dutch form; short forms are Derry, Rick, Rickie, Del and Dell.

Dermot *m*
(Irish); this is the anglicized version of the Irish name Diarmaid or Diarmait.

Derry *m*

(Irish); oak wood; a place name used as a first name.

Derwent *m*
(Old English); river flowing through oak woods; a place name and surname used as a first name.

Desdemona *f*
The name of the heroine in Shakespeare's *Othello*.

Désirée *f*
(French); meaning 'desired'.

Desmond *m*
(Irish); the meaning is derived from Desmond in Munster; short forms are Des and Desi.

Destiny *f*
A modern name which is popular in America.

Dev *m*
(Sanskrit); meaning 'god'.

Devdan *m*
(Sanskrit); gift from the gods.

Devlin *m*
(Irish); brave.

Devnet *f*
Another form of Dymphna.

Devon *m*
(Celtic); this name is probably derived from the county in England.

Dhanishta *f*
(Sanskrit); meaning 'a star'.

Diamond *f*
A modern name from the precious stone.

Diana *f*
(Latin); the name of the Roman goddess of the moon; the French form is Diane and the short form is Di; other related forms are Dianne and Deanna.

Dick *see* **Richard.**

Dido *f*
(Greek); meaning 'a teacher'.

Diego *m*
A Spanish name used in America, being a form of James.

Dietrich *m*
This name is the German form of Derek.

Digby *m*
(Old Norse); the village by the dike; a place name and a surname used as a first name.

Dilip *m*
(Sanskrit); the meaning is uncertain.

Dilys *f*
(Welsh); meaning 'genuine'; the short form is Dilly.

Dinah *f*
(Hebrew); meaning 'law suit'; another form is Dina and the short form is Di.

Dino *m*
(Italian); meaning 'small'.

Dion *m*
(Greek); like Denis, this name comes from Dionysos, the Greek god of wine.

Dionne *f*
(Greek); meaning 'a goddess'; another form is Dione.

Dirk *m*
The Dutch form of Derek.

Divya *f*
(Sanskrit); meaning 'heavenly radiance'.

Djamila *f*
The French form of Jamila.

Dolores *f*
(Spanish); a short form of the original meaning 'Mary of the Sorrows', short forms are Lola and Lolita.

Dolph *m*
This is a short form of Adolph.

Dominic *m*
(Latin); belonging to the Lord; another form is Dominick and the short form is Dom.

Dominique *f*
A French form of the Latin meaning 'of the Lord'; another form is Dominica.

Donal *m*
An Irish form of Donald.

Donald *m*
(Gaelic); mighty leader; short forms are Don and Donny.

Donalda *f*
The feminine form of Donald; another form is Donella.

Donata *f*
(Latin); meaning 'given'.

Donatus *m*
(Latin); gift from God.

Donna *f*

Doolan

(Italian); meaning 'a lady'.

Doolan *m*
(Irish); meaning 'defiance'; a surname used as a first name; another form is Dolan.

Dora *f*
This is a short form of Dorothy and Theodora which is now used as a separate name; the short form is Dorrie.

Doran *m*
(Irish); meaning 'stranger'; a surname used as a first name.

Dorcas *f*
(Greek); meaning 'a gazelle'.

Doreen *f*
This is probably an Irish version of Dorothy; another form is Dorinne and the short form is Dorrie.

Dorian *m*
(Greek); the name comes from an ancient people from the south of Greece; it was used by Oscar Wilde in The Picture of Dorian Gray; other forms are Dorien and Dorrien.

Dorianne *f*
The feminine form of Dorian; another form is Doriana.

Dorinda *f*
This name came into being as another version of Dorothy.

Doris *f*
The meaning is uncertain but the name was used in Greek mythology.

Dorothy *f*
(Greek); meaning 'gift of God'; another form is Dorothea and the short forms are Dolly, Dora, Dot, Dodie and Thea.

Dougal *m*

(Irish); dark stranger; other forms are Dugal and Dougall; the short form is Doug.

Douglas *m*

(Gaelic); meaning 'black stream'; a place name used as a first name; short forms are Doug, Dougie and Duggie.

Dow *m*

(Gaelic); black-haired; a surname used as a first name.

D'Oyley *m*

(Old French); a surname used as a first name.

Drake *m*

(Old English); a dragon; a surname used as a first name.

Drew *m*

(Old German); meaning 'to bear'; a surname used as a first name; Drew is also a short form of Andrew.

Driscel *m*

(Irish); a surname used as a first name.

Drummond *m*

A surname used as a first name.

Drury *m*

(Old French); beloved; a surname used as a first name.

Drusilla *f*

The feminine form of a Roman family name used as a first name.

Duane *m*

(Irish); meaning 'black'; other forms are Dwayne and Dewayne.

Dudley *m*

Duff

(Old English); the name comes from a place in Worcestershire.

Duff *m*
(Gaelic); swarthy; a surname used as a first name.

Duke *see* Marmaduke.

Dulcie *f*
(Latin); meaning 'sweet'; another form is Dulcibella, meaning 'sweet and lovely'.

Duncan *m*
(Gaelic); meaning 'brown'; originally a Scottish name but now used throughout the English-speaking world.

Dunn *m*
(Old English); dark-complexioned; a surname used as a first name.

Dunstane *m*
(Old English); meaning 'hill stone'.

Durga *f*
(Sanskrit); meaning 'out of reach'.

Durward *m*
A surname used as a first name.

Durwin *m*
(Old English); meaning 'a friend'; another form is Durwyn.

Dustin *m*
A name which is much used in America.

Dwight *m*
An English surname which is used as a first name, especially in America.

Dylan *m*

(Welsh); meaning 'son of the sea'; the name of the Welsh poet Dylan Thomas and used by the singer Bob Dylan.

Dymphna ƒ

(Irish); meaning 'a fawn'; another form is Devnet.

Eachan *m*

(Gaelic); a horseman; other forms are Eachaun and Eacheann.

Eamon *m*

(Irish); this name is the Irish form of Edmund; another form is Eamonn.

Earl *m*

(Old English); a nobleman; this is from the noble title and used as a first name, especially in America.

Eartha *f*

(Old English); meaning 'the earth'.

Easter *f*

The name of the Christain festival used as a first name.

Eaton *m*

A surname used as a first name.

Earnest *see* **Ernest.**

Ebenezer *m*

(Hebrew); stone of help; this name was used originally by the Puritans and is now mainly found in America; other forms are Eben and Eb.

Ebony *f*

The name of a very black wood used as a first name.

Ed *m*

Eda

A short form of Edgar, Edmund, Edwin and Edward.

Eda *see* **Edith.**

Edan *see* **Aidan.**

Edana *f*
Another form of Edna.

Edelmar *m*
(Old English); meaning 'noble'; the German form is Edel.

Eden *f*
(Hebrew); meaning 'gladness'.

Edgar *m*
(Old English); spear of fortune; short forms are Ed and Eddie.

Edith *f*
(Old English); meaning 'successful war'; another form is Editha and the short forms are Edie and Edy.

Edmund *m*
(Old English); protection of happiness; the short forms are Ed, Eddie, Ned and Ted; the French form is Edmond.

Edna *f*
The meaning of this name is unknown; another form is Edana.

Edric *m*
(Old English); meaning 'wealthy chief'.

Edward *m*
(Old English); happy guardian; a name much used by English kings; the short forms are Ted, Ned, Ed and Eddie.

Edwin *m*
(Old English); meaning 'friend'; the short form is Ed.

Edwina *f*
(Old English); meaning 'rich friend'; the feminine form of Edwin.

Effie *f*
A short form of Euphemia.

Egan *m*
(Irish); a surname used as a first name.

Egbert *m*
(Old German); bright sword; the short form is Bert.

Eglentyne *f*
(Old French); meaning 'prickly'; another form is Eglantine.

Eileen *f*
The Irish form of Evelyn; another form is Aileen and a short form is Eily.

Eilidh *f*
A Gaelic form of Helen.

Eilir *m*
(Welsh); a butterfly.

Eithne *f*
(Irish); meaning 'fire'; other forms are Ethne, Ethna and Aithne.

Ekata *f*
(Sanskrit); meaning 'harmony'.

Elaine *f*
A French form of Helen.

Elder *m*
(Old English); a senior person; a surname which is used as a first name.

Eldon *m*
A surname used as a first name.

Eleanor *f*
This is another Old French form of Helen which has been used in Britain for hundreds of years; another form is Elinor and the Italian forms are Eleanora and Leonora; the short forms are Ellie, Ella, Nell and Nora.

Eleazer *m*
(Hebrew); helped by God.

Elfed *m*
(Welsh); autumn.

Elfleda *f*
(Old English); meaning 'noble beauty'.

Elfreda *f*
A feminine form of Alfred; another form is Alfreda.

Elgiva *f*
(Old English); meaning 'noble gift'.

Eli *m*
(Hebrew); raised on high; this name is also a short form of Elias.

Elias *m*
(Hebrew); meaning 'Jehovah is God'; another form is Elijah.

Elin *f*
A Welsh form of Helen.

Elissa *f*
A short form of Elizabeth.

Elizabeth *f*
(Hebrew); meaning 'my God is fulfilment'; another form is

Elisabeth and there are many short forms such as Bess, Bessie, Beth, Betty, Eliza, Lizzy, Liz, Liza and Libby; Scottish versions are Elspeth and Elsie and European forms are Elsa, Elissa and Lisa (German), Bettina (Italian) and Elise, Lisette and Babette (French).

Elke *f*
A German short form of Alice.

Ellen *f*
Another form of Helen.

Elliot *m*
A surname used as a first name, derived from Elias.

Ellis *m*
A surname used as a first name.

Ellison *m*
(Old English); son of Elias; a surname used as a first name.

Elma *f*
A combination of parts of Elizabeth and Mary.

Elmer *m*
(Old English); noble defender; a surname used as a first name, especially in America; another form is Aylmer.

Elmore *m*
(Old English); river bank; a surname used as a first name.

Eloise *f*
The meaning of this name is uncertain; another form is Heloise; Abelard and Heloise were tragic lovers in the 12th century.

Elsa *f*
A short form of Elizabeth; another form is Elsie.

Elspeth *f*
A Scottish form of Elizabeth.

Elton *m*
(Old English); a surname used as a first name; the name was made known by the singer Elton John.

Eluned *f*
(Welsh); meaning 'idol'.

Elva *f*
(Old English); meaning 'the elf's friend'; another form is Elvina.

Elvin *m*
(Old English); noble friend; a surname used as a first name; another form is Elwin.

Elvira *f*
This is a Spanish name, the meaning of which is unknown.

Elvis *m*
This is a name made famous by Elvis Presley.

Emanuel *m*
(Hebrew); God with us; this was the name given by the prophet Isaiah to the Messiah; the short form is Manny.

Emeline *f*
Another form of Amelia.

Emer *f*
This is a name which comes from Irish legend.

Emerald *f*
The name of a gem used as a first name.

Emily *f*
The name of a Roman family used as a first name; the Italian

form is Emilia and the short forms are Emma and Millie; the French form Emmeline is sometimes used. In the top ten of popular girls' names.

Emlyn *m*
This name is possibly derived from a Welsh place name and is much used in Wales.

Emma *f*
(Old German); meaning 'universal'; the short form is Emmie. In the top twenty of popular girls' names.

Emmeline *f*
Another form of Emeline.

Emmett *m*
This is a surname used as a first name; other forms are Emmet, Emmot and Emmott.

Emrys *m*
A Welsh form of Ambrose.

Ena *f*
This is an English form of the Irish name Eithne and is also a short form of many other names ending in 'ena' and 'ina'.

Enfys *f*
(Welsh); meaning 'a rainbow'.

Engelbert *m*
(Old German); meaning 'angel'.

Engelberta *f*
The feminine form of Engelbert; another form is Engelbertha.

Enid *f*
(Welsh); meaning 'the spirit'.

Ennis *m*

Enoch

(Gaelic); meaning 'leader'.

Enoch *m*
(Hebrew); skilled or dedicated.

Eoghan *m*
(Irish); an Irish form of Eugene.

Eoin *m*
(Irish); an Irish form of John.

Ephraim *m*
(Hebrew); meaning 'fruitful'; this name is still used in America; the short form is Eph.

Erasmus *m*
(Greek); beloved; another form is Erastus and the short forms are Ras and Rastus.

Eric *m*
The name was brought to Britain by the Danes and is thought to mean 'ruler'; another form is Erik and the short forms are Rick, Rickie and Ricky.

Erica *f*
The feminine form of Eric; another form is Erika.

Erin *f*
(Irish); the poetic name for Ireland used as a first name.

Erle *see* **Earl.**

Ermyntrude *f*
(Old German); meaning 'universal strength'.

Ernest *m*
(Old German); earnestness; short forms are Ern and Ernie.

Ernestine *f*
The feminine form of Ernest.

Errol *m*
This is a surname used as a first name.

Erskine *m*
A place name and surname used as a first name.

Erwin *m*
(Old German); honourable friend; a surname used as a first name.

Esau *m*
(Hebrew); meaning 'hairy'.

Esmé *f*
(French); meaning 'loved'; other forms are Esmée, and Esma and a very similar name is the French Aimée.

Esmeralda *f*
The Spanish form of Emerald; another form is Esmeraldah.

Esmond *m*
(Old English); protection from above.

Estelle *f*
(French); meaning 'a star'; another form is Estella.

Esther *f*
(Persian); meaning 'myrtle'; other forms are Ester and Hester and the short forms are Essy, Essie, Ess, Tess and Hettie.

Estrild *f*
(Old English); meaning 'goddess of the rising sun'.

Etain *f*
This is a name from Irish legend; other forms are Etan and Eadan.

Ethan *m*
(Hebrew); meaning 'firm'; more common in America.

Ethel *f*
(Old English); meaning 'of high birth'.

Ethna *f*
An English form of Eithne.

Etienne *m*
Is the French form of Stephen.

Etta *f*
A short form of Henrietta; another form is Ettie.

Euan *m*
Is another form of Ewan.

Eugene *m*
(Greek); meaning 'well-born'; the Irish form of this name is
Eoghan or Eoan and the Scottish forms are Ewan, Ewen or
Euan; the short form in America is Gene.

Eugenie *f*
(Greek); meaning 'high-born'; this is the feminine form of
Eugene; another form is Eugenia.

Eulalia *f*
(Greek); meaning 'speaking sweetly'.

Eunice *f*
(Greek); meaning 'joyous victory'.

Euphemia *f*
(Greek); meaning 'favourable speech'; other forms are
Eufemia and Euphemie and the short forms are Effie, Fay and
Phoebe.

Eustace *m*
(Greek); fruitful; short forms are Stacey and Stacy.

Eustacia *f*

The feminine form of Eustace; the short form Stacey is now used as a separate name.

Eva *see* **Eve.**

Evadne *f*
This is a Greek name, the meaning of which is unclear.

Evan *m*
(Welsh); this name is a Welsh form of John.

Evangeline *f*
(Greek); meaning 'belonging to the Gospels'.

Eve *f*
(Hebrew); meaning 'lively'; another form is Eva and the short forms are Evie and Evita (Spanish); other associated names are Eveline, Eveleen and Evelina.

Evelyn *m* and *f*
This is a surname used as a first name.

Everard *m*
(Old German); meaning 'brave boar'; the Scottish form is Ewart.

Everett *m*
A surname derived from Everard which is used as a first name.

Ewan *m*
This is a Scottish form of Eugene; other forms are Euan and Owen.

Ezekiel *m*
(Hebrew); strengthened by God; the short form is Zeke.

Ezra *m*
Hebrew); meaning 'help'.

Fabia *f*
The feminine form of Fabio; another form is Fabiola.

Fabian *m*
(Latin); meaning 'a bean'; this is the anglicized form of a Roman family name.

Fabio *m*
Is the Italian form of Fabian.

Fahimah *f*
(Arabic); meaning 'astute'.

Faisal *m*
(Arabic); meaning 'a judge'; this name has been used as a royal name in both Iraq and Saudi Arabia; other forms are Feisal and Faysal.

Fairley *m*
A surname used as a first name; another form is Fairlie.

Faith *f*
A Christian virtue used as a first name; the short forms are Fay and Faye.

Fane *m*
(Old English); meaning 'glad'; a surname used as a first name.

Fanny *f*

Farah

A short form of Frances.

Farah *f*
(Arabic); meaning 'joy'; another form is Farrah.

Farhanah *f*
(Arabic); meaning 'overjoyed'.

Farnall *m*
A surname used as a first name; another form is Farnell.

Farquhar *m*
(Gaelic); meaning 'dear man'; a surname used as a first name.

Farr *m*
A surname used as a first name.

Farrell *m*
(Irish); a warrior.

Fatima *f*
(Arabic); meaning 'chaste'.

Faustine *f*
(Latin); meaning 'favoured'; another form is Fausta.

Fawn *f*
The name for a young deer used as a first name.

Fay *f*
This is a short form of Faith and Euphemia; another form is
Faye.

Felicia *f*
(Latin); meaning 'happy'; this is the feminine form of Felix;
another form is Felice.

Felicity *f*
(Latin); meaning 'happiness'; a short form is Felly.

Felix *m*

(Latin); meaning 'happy'.

Felton *m*

(Old English); meaning 'a field'; a place name and surname used as a first name.

Fenella *f*

(Gaelic); meaning 'white-shouldered'; another form is Finola.

Fenton *m*

(Old English); meaning 'a marsh'; a place name and surname used as a first name.

Ferdinand *m*

(Old German); meaning 'bold journey'; the short forms are Ferd and Ferdie.

Fergal *m*

(Irish); meaning 'brave'; the short forms are Fergie and Fergy.

Fergus *m*

(Irish); meaning 'strong man'; a common name in Scotland and Ireland; the short form is Fergie.

Ferguson *m*

Meaning 'son of Fergus'; this is a surname used as a first name.

Fern *f*

The name of a plant used as a first name.

Fernand *m*

This name is a French form of Ferdinand.

Ffion *f*

(Welsh); meaning 'the foxglove'.

Fi *see* **Fiona.**

Fidel *m*
A Spanish form of Fidelis.

Fidelis *m* and *f*
(Latin); meaning 'faithful'; another *f* form is Fidelia

Fidelma *f*
An Irish name, the meaning of which is unknown.

Fielding *m*
A surname used as a first name.

Fifi *f*
A French short form of Josephine.

Fingal *m*
(Gaelic); blond stranger; the name of a Scottish hero of legend; his name was given to Fingal's Cave.

Finlay *m*
(Gaelic); meaning 'a fair-haired warrior'; another form is Findlay.

Finn *m*
(Irish); meaning 'fair-haired'; this name is similar to the Scottish Fingal; it can also be used as a short form of Finbar.

Fiona *f*
(Gaelic); meaning 'fair and white'; the short form is Fi.

Fionnuala *f*
(Irish); meaning 'white-shouldered'; a short form is Nuala.

Fiske *m*
(Old English); meaning 'a fish'; a surname used as a first name.

Fitch *m*
A surname used as a first name.

Fitz *m*

(Old French); meaning 'son'; this name is used for a prefix for many surnames such as Fitzpatrick (son of Patrick) and Fitzroy (son of the king).

Flann *m*

(Irish); meaning 'red-haired'; it was probably used originally as a nickname.

Flavia *f*

(Latin); meaning 'yellow'; a Roman family name used as a first name.

Fleming *m*

(Old French); a man from Flanders; a surname used as a first name.

Fletcher *m*

A surname used as a first name.

Fleur *f*

(French); meaning 'a flower'; the English forms are Flower and Blossom.

Flint *m*

(Old English); meaning 'a stream'.

Flora *f*

(Latin); meaning 'flower'.

Florence *f*

(Latin); meaning 'blooming'; short forms are Flo, Florrie and Flossie.

Florian *m*

(Latin); derived from the word meaning 'blooming'; another form is Florent.

Floyd *m*

Another form of Lloyd (Welsh) meaning 'grey'.

Forbes *m*
(Gaelic); meaning 'fields'; a place name and a surname used as a first name.

Forrest *m*
This is a surname used as a first name which originated in the United States.

Fortune *f*
This word is sometimes used as a first name.

Foster *m*
(Old French); a forester; a surname used as a first name.

Frances *f*
Derived from the Italian name Francesca; two French forms are Francine and Françoise and the short forms are Fran, Francie, Fanny and Frankie.

Francis *m*
(Latin); meaning 'a Frenchman'; the short forms are Frank, Frankie and Fran.

François *m*
The French form of Francis.

Frank *m*
A short form of Francis which can also be used as a separate name.

Franklyn *m*
A surname used as a first name; another form is Franklin.

Fraser *m*
A Scottish surname used as a first name; another form is Frazer.

Frayn *m*
(Old French); an ash tree; a surname used as a first name.

Frederica *f*
The feminine form of Frederick; the short forms are Freda, Frida and Frieda.

Frederick *m*
(Old German); peaceful ruler; other forms are Frederik and Frederic and the short forms are Fred, Freddie and Freddy.

Freeman *m*
(Old English); a free man; a surname used as a first name.

Freya *f*
The name of the Norse goddess of love; other forms are Frea and Freja.

Fulton *m*
A surname used as a first name.

Fulvia *f*
The feminine form of a Roman family name used as a first name.

Fyfe *m*
A surname meaning from Fife in Scotland used as a first name. Another form is Fyffe.

Gabriel *m*
(Hebrew); strong man of God; this is the name of one of the
Archangels; a short form is Gabe.

Gabrielle *f*
The feminine form of Gabriel; another form is Gabriella and
the short forms are Gaby and Gabby.

Gaia *f*
The name of the goddess of the earth in Greek mythology;

Gail *f*
A short form of Abigail which is now used as a separate
name; other forms are Gale and Gayle.

Gallagher *m*
(Irish); a surname used as a first name.

Galloway *m*
A place name and a surname used as a first name.

Galvin *m*
(Irish); meaning 'bright'.

Gamaliel *m*
(Hebrew); my recompense is God.

Ganesh *m*
(Sanskrit); lord of the hosts.

Gardenia *f*

Gareth

The name of the plant used as a first name.

Gareth *m*
(Welsh); meaning 'gentle'; the short forms are Gary and Garry; another form is Garth.

Garfield *m*
(Old English); a field shaped as a spear; a surname used as a first name.

Garland *f*
The name for a wreath used as a first name.

Garnet *m* and *f*
A surname and the name of a gem used as a first name; another form is Garnett.

Garret *m*
This is the Irish form of Gerard; another form is Garrett.

Garrison *m*
A surname used as a first name.

Garry *m*
This is another form of Gary, which is derived from an American place name.

Garth *m*
(Old Norse); a paddock; a surname used as a first name; it is also another form of Gareth.

Garton *m*
A surname used as a first name.

Garve *m*
A place name in Scotland used as a first name.

Gary *m*
This was the stage name of Gary Cooper which was chosen

from the American town of that name; it can also be used as the short form of Gareth and Garfield.

Gaspard *m*
This name is the French form of Jasper.

Gaston *m*
(French); meaning a man from Gascony.

Gauri *f*
(Sanskrit); meaning 'white'.

Gavin *m*
(Old French); the name was Gauvin in French; it is known as Gavin in Scotland and is now used worldwide.

Gay *f*
The name meaning 'happy' used as a first name; another form is Gaye.

Gaylord *m*
A surname used as a first name.

Gaynor *f*
Another form of Guinevere and Jennifer.

Gemma *f*
(Italian); meaning 'a gem'; another form is Jemma.

Gene *m*
A short form of Eugene which can also be used as a separate name.

Genevieve *f*
(Old French); the meaning is uncertain; the short forms are Gina and Ginette.

Geoffrey *m*
(Old German); perhaps meaning 'peace'; an alternative form

of Jeffrey; the short form is Geoff.

George *m*

(Greek); meaning 'a farmer'; St. George is the patron saint of England; the short forms are Geordie, Georgie and Georgy; in the top twenty of popular boys' names.

Georges *m*

Is the French form of George.

Georgina *f*

The feminine form of George; other forms are Georgia, Georgiana and Georgette. In the top twenty of popular girls' names.

Geraint *m*

(Welsh); meaning 'old'.

Gerald *m*

(Old German); chief with a spear; the short forms are Gerry and Jerry.

Geraldine *f*

The feminine form of Gerald.

Gerard *m*

(Old German); courageous with a spear; the short forms are Gerry and Jerry.

Gerda *f*

A name from Norse mythology.

Germain *m*

A name which probably originally meant a German.

Germaine *f*

Possibly the meaning is 'a German'.

Gerry *f*

A short form of Geraldine.

Gertrude *f*
(Old German); meaning 'spear of strength'; the short forms are Gert, Gertie, Trudy, Trudie and Trudi.

Gervais *m*
(Old German); spear carrier.

Ghislaine *f*
(Old French); meaning 'word of honour'; other forms are Ghislane and Ghislain.

Giacomo *m*
The Italian form of James.

Gianna *f*
A short form of Giovanna; other forms are Gina and Vanna.

Gibson *m*
A surname used as a first name.

Gideon *m*
(Hebrew); a hewer; the name of a great leader of Israel; it was used by the Puritans, who took it to America, where it is still used.

Giffard *m*
A surname used as a first name; another form is Gifford.

Gigi *f*
A French short form of Gilberte.

Gilbert *m*
(Old German); meaning 'bright'; the short forms are Gib, Bert and Bertie.

Gilberta *f*
The feminine form of Gilbert; the short forms are Gill and

Gilly.

Gilchrist *m*
(Gaelic); Christ's servant; the short form is Gil.

Gilda *f*
(Old German); meaning 'offering'.

Giles *m*
(Greek); meaning 'goatskin'; the short form is Gil.

Gilles *m*
Is the French form of Giles.

Gillespie *m*
A surname used as a first name.

Gillian *f*
The English form of Juliana; another form is Jillian and the short forms are Gill, Gilly, Jill and Jilly.

Gilmour *m*
A surname used as a first name; other forms are Gilmore and Gillmore.

Gilroy *m*
A surname used as a first name.

Gina *f*
A short form of Genevieve which is now used as a separate name.

Ginette *see* **Genevieve.**

Ginevra *f*
The Italian form of Genevieve.

Giraldo *m*
The Italian form of Gerald.

Giraud *m*
The French form of Gerald.

Girvan *m*
A Scottish place name used as a first name.

Giselle *f*
(Old German); meaning 'a promise'; another form is Gisela.

Gita *f*
(Sanskrit); meaning 'a song'; another form is Geeta.

Githa *f*
(Old Norse); meaning 'war'; another form is Gytha.

Gladwin *m*
(Old English); glad friend; a surname used as a first name.

Gladys *f*
The English form of a Welsh version of Claudia; the short form is Glad.

Glanville *m*
(Old French); living among oak trees; another form is Glanvil.

Glen *m*
(Gaelic); a valley; another form is Glenn.

Glenda *f*
(Welsh); meaning 'good'; other forms are Glenys, Glynis and Glyn.

Glenna *f*
(Celtic); meaning 'a valley'.

Gloria *f*
(Latin); meaning 'glory'.

Glyn *m*

Goddard

(Welsh); a valley; another form is Glynn.

Goddard *m*
(Old German); meaning 'a hard God'; now used mainly as a surname.

Godfrey *m*
(Old German); the peace of God.

Godiva *f*
(Old English); meaning 'a gift'.

Godric *m*
(Old English); God the ruler.

Godwin *m*
(Old English); the friend of God.

Golda *f*
(Hebrew); meaning 'gold'.

Goldwin *m*
(Old English); friend of gold.

Goodwin *m*
A surname used as a first name.

Gopal *m*
(Sanskrit); a worshiper of Krishna; another form is Gopalkrishna.

Gordon *m*
A Scottish place name used as a first name; it is also the name of a famous clan in Scotland.

Govind *m*
A name with the same derivation as Gopal; a Sikh form is Gobind.

Grace *f*

(Latin); meaning 'grace'; the short form is Gracie.

Grady *m*
(Irish); a surname used as a first name.

Graham *m*
A Scottish surname used as a first name; other forms are Graeme and Grahame.

Grainne *f*
The name of a princess from Celtic legend; another form is Grania.

Granger *m*
A surname used as a first name.

Grant *m*
From the French meaning tall or large, this is a Scottish surname used as a first name.

Granville *m*
(Old French); a large town.

Gray *m*
(Old English); meaning grey-haired; a surname used as a first name; another form is Grey.

Gregory *m*
(Greek); a watchman; the Scottish version is Gregor and the short form is Greg.

Gresham *m*
A surname used as a first name.

Greta *f*
A Swedish short form of Margaret; short forms are Gretel and Gretchen.

Greville *m*

Grier

A surname from France used as a first name.

Grier *m*
A surname used as a first name.

Griffith *m*
(Welsh); strong warrior; the Welsh form is Gruffydd and the short form is Griff.

Griselda *f*
(Old German); the meaning is doubtful; other forms are Grizel and Zelda.

Grover *m*
A surname used as a first name.

Gudrun *f*
(Old Norse); meaning 'the secret of God'.

Guido *m*
The Italian and Spanish forms of Guy.

Guinevere *f*
(Welsh); meaning 'white'; the name of King Arthur's wife in legend.

Gulab *m* and *f*
(Sanskrit); meaning 'a rose'.

Gunter *m*
(Old German); bold in war.

Gus *m*
A short form of both Angus and Augustus.

Gustav *m*
(Old Norse); this name was used by Swedish kings and is still in use in America; the French form is Gustave; a short form is Gus.

Guthrie *m*

A surname used as a first name.

Guy *m*

(Old German); the meaning is uncertain; a French form is Guyon.

Gwendolen *f*

(Welsh); meaning 'white circle'; other forms are Gwendolyn and Gwendolin and the short forms are Gwen and Gwenda.

Gwyn *m*

(Welsh); blessed or fair; another form is Gwynn.

Gwyneth *f*

(Welsh); meaning 'joy'; the short form is Gwyn.

Gwynfor *m*

(Welsh); fair and great.

H

Haakon *m*
(Old Norse); meaning 'useful'; another form is Hakon.

Haddon *m*
A surname used as a first name.

Hadley *m*
A surname used as a first name.

Hadrian *see* Adrian.

Hagley *m*
A surname used as a first name.

Haidee *f*
(Greek); meaning 'embraceable'.

Haig *m*
(Old English); a surname used as a first name.

Hal *m*
A short form of Henry and Halbert.

Halbert *see* Albert.

Hale *m*
A surname used as a first name.

Hall *m*
(Old English); living in the manor house; a surname used as a first name.

Hallam *m*
(Old English); the hollow; a surname used as a first name.

Halstead *m*
A surname used as a first name.

Hamilton *m*
A surname used as a first name.

Hamish *m*
(Gaelic); this is the Gaelic form of James, which is used mainly in Scotland.

Hamlet *m*
(Old German); meaning 'small house'; a surname used as a first name; another form is Hamlett.

Hamon *m*
(Old German); a home.

Hamzah *m*
(Arabic); a lion; another form is Hamza.

Hana *f*
(Arabic); meaning 'joyfulness'.

Hanford *m*
A surname used as a first name.

Hani *m*
(Arabic); meaning 'happiness'.

Hank *see* Henry.

Hanley *m*
A surname used as a first name.

Hannah *f*
(Hebrew); meaning 'God has favoured me'; another form is Ann; in the top twenty of popular girls' names.

Hans *m*
The German form of John, being derived from Johannes.

Harden *m*
A surname used as a first name.

Hardy *m*
(Old German); meaning 'courageous'; a surname used as a first name; other forms are Hardie and Hardey.

Hargreave *m*
A surname used as a first name; other forms are Hargreaves and Hargrave.

Hari *m*
(Sanskrit); meaning 'light brown'.

Harley *m*
A surname used as a first name.

Harlow *m*
(Old English); a fortified hill; a place name and a surname used as a first name.

Harmony *f*
This expressive word is used as a first name.

Harold *m*
(Old English); power of an army; the short form is Harry.

Harriet *f*
The feminine form of Henry or Harry; the short forms are Hattie and Hatty.

Harrison *m*
Meaning 'son of Harry'; this is a surname used as a first name.

Harry *m*

A short form of Henry which is also a separate name; in the top twenty of popular boys' names.

Harsha *f*
(Sanskrit); meaning 'happiness'.

Harun *m*
(Arabic); this name is probably from the same derivation as Aaron; another form is Haroun.

Harvey *m*
(Old French); meaning 'ready for battle'; this is a surname used as a first name; other forms are Hervey and Harvie.

Hasan *m*
(Arabic); meaning 'good'; this is one of the most popular Muslim names; other forms are Hassan, Hussain and Hussein.

Hastings *m*
A place name and a surname used as a first name.

Havelock *m*
Is said to be the Welsh form of Oliver.

Hawley *m*
A surname used as a first name.

Hayden *m*
A surname used as a first name; another form is Haydon.

Hayley *m* and *f*
(Old English); a hay field; other forms are Haley and Haylie.

Haywood *m*
A surname used as a first name; another form is Heywood.

Hazel *f*
The name of a tree used as a first name.

Hazlett *m*
(Old English); hazel tree; a surname used as a first name; other forms are Hazlitt and Haslett.

Heath *m*
A surname used as a first name.

Heathcliff *m*
(Old English); living by the cliff of heather; another form is Heathcliffe.

Heather *f*
The name of a plant used as a first name.

Hebe *f*
(Greek); the name of the goddess of youth in Greek mythology.

Hector *m*
(Greek); hold fast; this is a name which has been popular in Scotland.

Hedda *f*
(Old German); meaning 'warfare'.

Heidi *f*
A short form of the German version of Adelaide.

Helen *f*
(Greek); meaning 'the bright one'; other forms are Elena, Elaine and Ellen and the short forms are Lena, Nell and Ilona.

Helga *f*
(Old Norse); meaning 'holy'.

Hema *f*
(Sanskrit); meaning 'golden'.

Hendrik *m*
The Dutch form of Henry.

Henri *m*
The French form of Henry.

Henrietta *f*
The feminine form of Henry; a derived form is Harriet and the short forms are Etta, Ettie, Hetty, Netta and Nettie.

Henry *m*
(Old German); the head of a house; the short forms are Harry, Hal and Hank.

Hephzibah *f*
(Hebrew); meaning 'my delight is in her'.

Herbert *m*
(Old German); gleaming army; the short forms are Herb, Herbie, Bert and Bertie.

Hereward *m*
(Old English); meaning 'army guard'.

Herman *m*
(Old German); a soldier; the French form is Armand; another form is Hermann.

Hermia *f*
(Greek); a feminine form of Hermes, the messenger of the gods in Greek mythology.

Hermione *f*
(Greek); this is another name from Greek mythology meaning 'daughter of Hermes'.

Hermosa *f*
(Spanish); meaning 'lovely'.

Hernando *m*
Is the Spanish form of Ferdinand.

Herta *f*
(Old English); meaning 'from the earth'.

Hesketh *m*
A surname used as a first name.

Hester *f*
Another form of Esther.

Hew *see* **Hugh.**

Hewett *m*
A surname used as a first name; another form is Hewit.

Hezekiah *m*
(Hebrew); God is strength.

Hibernia *f*
(Latin); the name of Ireland used as a first name.

Hibiscus *f*
The name of a plant used as a first name.

Hilaire *m*
The French form of Hilary.

Hilary *m* and *f*
(Latin); meaning 'merry or cheerful'; another form is Hillary.

Hilda *f*
(Old English); meaning 'battle'; another form is Hylda.

Hildebrand *m* and *f*
(Old German); battle sword.

Hildegarde *f*
(Old German); meaning 'warfare'.

Hilton *m*
A surname used as a first name.

Hina *f*
(Sanskrit); meaning 'henna' the dye.

Hiram *m*
(Hebrew); my brother on high; another form is Hyram.

Holbrook *m*
A surname used as a first name.

Holden *m*
A surname used as a first name.

Hollis *m*
A surname used as a first name.

Holly *f*
The name of the tree used as a first name.

Holmes *m*
A surname used as a first name.

Homer *m*
Is the name of the Greek poet; it is more often used as a first name in the United States.

Honey *f*
The name of the substance made from nectar used as a first name.

Honoria *f*
(Latin); meaning 'reputation'; another form is Honora; the short form is Nora, also used as a separate name.

Honour *f*
The word for integrity used as a first name.

Hope *f*

The Christian virtue used as a first name.

Horace *m*
This name comes from the Roman family Horatius; another form is Horatio.

Horatia *f*
The feminine form of Horace.

Houghton *m*
A surname used as a first name; another form is Hutton.

Houston *m*
A surname used as a first name.

Howard *m*
An aristocratic surname which for many years has been used as a first name; a short form is Howie.

Howell *m*
(Welsh); meaning 'eminent'; other forms are Howel and Hywel.

Hubert *m*
(Old German); bright mind; the short form is Bert.

Hudson *m*
A surname used as a first name.

Hugh *m*
(Old German); meaning 'heart' or 'mind'; the Latin form is Hugo and Welsh forms are Hew and Huw; the short forms are Hughie and Huey and Shug in Scotland.

Hulda *f*
(Norse); meaning 'covered'.

Huldah *f*
(Hebrew); meaning 'a weasel'; the name of a prophetess.

Humbert *m*

(Old German); bright giant.

Humphrey *m*

(Old English); meaning 'peace'; another form is Humphry and the short form is Humph.

Hunter *m*

(Old English); a hunter; a surname used as a first name.

Huntley *m*

A surname used as a first name; another form is Huntly.

Huxley *m*

A surname used as a first name.

Hyacinth *f*

The name of the flower used as a first name.

Hyam *m*

(Hebrew); a man full of life; another form is Hyman.

Hywel *m*

The Welsh form of Howell.

Ian *see* **John.**

Iain *see* **John.**

Ianthe *f*
(Greek); meaning 'violet flower'.

Ida *f*
(Old German); meaning 'hard-working'.

Idonea *f*
(Old Norse); possibly meaning 'work'.

Idony *f*
(Old Norse); a name coming from Norse legend.

Idris *m*
Welsh); fiery lord.

Ifor *m*
The Welsh form of Ivor.

Ignatia *f*
The feminine form of Ignatius.

Ignatius *m*
(Greek); meaning is uncertain but possibly 'fiery'; the French form is Ignace.

Igor *m*
(Scandinavian); this is a name much used in Russia.

Ike *see* **Isaac.**

Ilona *f*
A Hungarian form of Helen.

Ilse *f*
A short form of Elisabeth.

Imelda *f*
A name of obscure origin which came into use this century.

Immanuel *m*
Another form of Emmanuel.

Imogen *f*
This name may have been a misprint of Innogen in Shakespeare's *Cymbeline*.

Ina *f*
A short form of names ending in –ina; it is also another form of Ena.

Inderjit *m*
(Sanskrit); conqueror of the god Indra.

India *f*
The name of the country used as a first name.

Indira *f*
(Sanskrit); meaning 'loveliness'.

Indra *f*
(Sanskrit); meaning 'a raindrop'.

Inez *f*
A Spanish form of Agnes.

Inga *f*
A short form of Ingeborg and Ingrid.

Ingeborg *f*
(Old Norse); meaning 'Ing's fortress'; Ing was the god of fertility in Norse legend.

Ingemar *m*
(Old Norse); son of Ing; another form is Ingmar and the short form is Inge.

Ingram *m*
Old German); angel raven; a surname used as a first name.

Ingrid *f*
(Old Norse); meaning 'belonging to Ing', the god of fertility.

Inigo *m*
Another form of Ignatius which is now used as an independent name.

Innes *m*
A surname used as a first name; another form is Inness.

Iola *f*
(Greek); meaning 'a cloud at dawn'; another form is Iole.

Iolanthe *f*
(Greek); meaning 'violet flower'.

Iona *f*
The name of the Scottish island used as a first name.

Iorwerth *m*
(Welsh); a nobleman of worth; short forms are Iolo and Iolyn.

Ira *m*
Aramaic); meaning 'watchful'.

Irene *f*
(Greek); meaning 'peace'; another form is Irena and the short

forms are Renie and Rene.

Iris *f*
(Greek); meaning 'the rainbow'.

Irma *f*
(German); meaning 'ubiquitous'.

Irvine *m*
A surname used as a first name; another form is Irving.

Irwin *m*
(Old English); meaning 'a friend of the boars'; a surname used as a first name.

Isaac *m*
(Hebrew); meaning 'laughter'; another form is Izaak and the short form is Ike.

Isabel *f*
This is another form of Elizabeth; other forms are Isabelle, Isobel, Iseabail and Ishbel (Gaelic) and Isabella; the short forms are Isa, Bel, Belle and Bella.

Isadora *f*
(Greek); possibly meaning 'a gift'; another form is Isidora.

Isaiah *m*
(Hebrew); meaning 'Jehovah is generous'.

Isidore *m*
Greek); probably meaning 'a gift'.

Isla *f*
A Scottish island name used as a first name; another form is Islay.

Ismail *m*
The Arabic form of Ishmael.

Isolda *f*
(Old Welsh); meaning 'beautiful one'; other forms are Iseult, Isolde, Yseult and Ysolde.

Israel *m*
(Hebrew); possibly 'may God prevail'; a short form is Izzy.

Istvan *m*
The Hungarian form of Stephen.

Ivan *m*
The Russian form of John.

Ivana *f*
The feminine form of Ivan.

Ivor *m*
This is the English form of the Welsh name Ifor.

Ivy *f*
The name of the plant used as a first name.

Jabez *m*
(Hebrew); meaning uncertain.

Jacinth *f*
The name of a precious stone used as a first name; this name is related to Hyacinth.

Jack *m*
A short form of John which is now used independantly; the short forms are Jackie and Jacky. In the top ten of popular boys' names.

Jackson *m*
The name means 'the son of Jack'; a surname used as a first name.

Jacob *m*
(Hebrew); the meaning is uncertain; the short form is Jake, which can be used as an independent name.

Jacoba *f*
The feminine form of Jacob; other forms are Jacobine and Jacobina.

Jacqueline *f*
The feminine form of Jacques, the French form of James; other forms are Jacquetta, Jacaline, Jacquelyn and Jaqueline; the short forms are Jacky, Jackie and Jacqui.

Jacques *m*

Jade

The French form of James.

Jade *f*
The name of the precious stone used as a first name.

Jael *f*
(Hebrew); meaning 'wild she-goat'.

Jalal *m*
(Arabic); meaning 'greatness'; other forms are Jalil, Galal and Galil.

Jalila *f*
(Arabic); meaning 'greatness'; another form is Galila.

Jamal *m*
(Arabic); meaning 'beautiful'; other forms are Jaimal, Jamil and Jamel.

James *m*
(Hebrew); this name is from the same background as Jacob; the short forms are Jim, Jimmy and Jamie. In the top ten of popular boys' names.

Jamesina *f*
The feminine form of James.

Jamie *f*
A short form of James which is used as a name for girls and boys.

Jamila *f*
(Arabic); meaning 'lovely'; the French form is Djamila.

Jan *m* and *f*
This is a short form of John (*m*) and Janet (*f*) and is also the Dutch form of John.

Jane *f*

The feminine form of John; another form is Jayne and the short forms are Jenny, Janey and Janie; related names are Janis and Jancis.

Janet *f*
Another form of Jane; other forms are Janette, Janetta and Jeanette; the short forms are Nettie, Netta and Jan.

Janine *f*
This is a name related to Jeanne, the French form of Jean; other forms are Jannine and Janene.

Jared *m*
This name comes from Arabic and Hebrew; other forms are Jarred, Jarod and Jarrod.

Jarvis *m*
This is a form of Gervais which became a surname and is also used as a first name.

Jasmine *f*
The name of a flower used as a first name; the Persian form is Yasmin, which can also be spelt Yasmine.

Jason *m*
(Hebrew); meaning 'the Lord saves'; in mythology the Greek hero who won the Golden Fleece.

Jasper *m*
The meaning is uncertain; other forms are Caspar or Gaspar – one of the three wise men who worshipped the infant Jesus in Bethlehem.

Javier *m*
A Spanish form of Xavier.

Jawahir *f*
(Arabic); meaning 'precious stones'.

Jay *m* and *f*

(Sanskrit); meaning 'victory'; also a short form of many names beginning with J.

Jean *f*

A Scottish form of Jane; the short forms are Jeanie and Jenny.

Jedidiah *m*

(Hebrew); meaning 'friend of the Lord'; the short form is Jed.

Jefferson *m*

Meaning 'son of Jeffrey'; a surname used as a first name.

Jeffrey *m*

(Old German); meaning 'peace'; see Geoffrey; the short form is Jeff.

Jemima *f*

(Hebrew); meaning 'a dove'; another form is Jemimah and the short forms are Mima and Mina.

Jennifer *f*

This is a Cornish form of Guenevere; another version is Genna and other forms of Guenevere are Gaenor and Gaynor; the short forms are Jenny and Jenni.

Jeremy *m*

(Hebrew); meaning 'may Jehovah raise up'; this name is a form of Jeremiah; the short form is Jerry.

Jermaine *f*

Another form of Germaine.

Jerome *m*

(Greek); meaning 'holy name'; a short form is Jerry.

Jerry *m*

This is a name which is used independently but is also the short form for Jerome, Jeremy, Gerald and Gerard.

Jervis *m*
Another form of Jarvis.

Jesse *m*
(Hebrew); meaning 'God lives'; short forms are Jess and Jake.

Jessica *f*
(Hebrew); meaning 'God beholds'; the short forms are Jess and Jessie. In the top ten of popular girls' names.

Jethro *m*
(Hebrew); meaning 'excellence'.

Jezebel *f*
(Hebrew); meaning 'supremacy'.

Jill *f*
A short form of Jillian and Gillian, now used as a separate name.

Jim, Jimmy *see* **James.**

Joab *m*
(Hebrew); meaning 'Jehovah is a father'.

Joachim *m*
(Hebrew); meaning 'may Jehovah exalt'.

Joan *f*
The oldest feminine form of John; another form is Joanne and the short forms are Joanie and Joni.

Job *m*
Hebrew); meaning 'persecuted'.

Jocelyn *m*
(Old German); possibly meaning 'little Goth'; short forms are Jos and Joss.

Jocelyn *f*

Jock

(Latin); meaning 'happy'; another form is Jocelin.

Jock *m*
A Scottish short form of John and Jack; often used as a nickname for a Scotsman.

Jodie *f*
A short form of Judith now used as a separate name; another form is Jody.

Joel *m*
(Hebrew); meaning 'Jehovah is God'.

Johann *m*
A German form of John; the short form is Hans.

Johanna *f*
The German form of Jane.

John *m*
(Hebrew); meaning 'Jehovah is gracious'; first used in the Latin form Johannes; there are many short forms – Jack, Jackie, Johnnie, Johnny, Jan and Jock; also derived from this name are the Gaelic Ian and Iain, the Welsh Evan and the Irish Eoin or Sean.

Jolyon *m*
Another form of Julian.

Jonah *m*
(Hebrew); meaning 'dove'; another form is Jonas.

Jonathan *m*
(Hebrew); meaning 'Jehovah has given'; another form is Jonathon and the short form is Jon.

Jordan *m* and *f*
(Hebrew); meaning 'flowing down'; this is now a popular name and is in the top twenty favourite names for boys.

Jos *m*
A short form of Joseph and Jocelyn.

Jose *m*
The Spanish form of Joseph.

Joseph *m*
(Hebrew); meaning 'Jehovah added'; short forms are Joe, Joeh and Jo. In the top twenty popular boys' names.

Josephine *f*
This is the French feminine form of Joseph; other forms are Josepha and Josephina and the short forms are Jo, Josie and, in France, Fifi.

Joshua *m*
(Hebrew); meaning 'God is generous'; the short form is Josh, which is now used as an independent name. In the top ten popular boys' names.

Josiah *m*
(Hebrew); meaning 'may Jehovah heal'; another form is Josias.

Jotham *m*
(Hebrew); meaning 'God is perfect'.

Joy *f*
The word for 'happiness' used as a first name.

Joyce *f*
A name which is used for both boys and girls.

Jude *m*
(Hebrew); possibly meaning 'Jehovah leads'; this is a short form of Judah; also derived from this name are Judas and Yehudi.

Judith *f*

Jules

(Hebrew); meaning 'a Jewess'; the short forms are Jodie, Jody and Judy, which is now used as a separate name.

Jules *see* **Julian.**

Julia *f*
The feminine form of Julius; the short forms are Julie and Juliet.

Julian *m*
This name is derived from the Roman family name Julius; other forms are Jolyon, Julyan and Jules; the French form is Julien.

Juliana *f*
The feminine form of Julian.

Junayd *m*
(Arabic); meaning 'a warrior'.

June *f*
The name of the month used as a first name.

Juno *f*
(Latin); the queen of heaven in Roman mythology.

Justin *m*
(Latin); meaning 'just'.

Justine *f*
(Latin); meaning 'just'; this is the feminine form of Justin; an older form is Justina.

K

Kamal *m*
(Sanskrit); meaning 'light red'.

Kamil *m*
(Arabic); meaning 'perfect'.

Kamila *f*
(Arabic); meaning 'perfect'; another form is Kamilah.

Kane *m*
A surname used as a first name.

Kanta *f*
(Sanskrit); meaning 'lovely'.

Kara *f*
Another form of Cara.

Karel *see* **Carol.**

Karen *f*
A Scandinavian form of Katharine; other forms are Karin and Karyn.

Karl *m*
A German form of Charles.

Karla *f*
The feminine form of Karl.

Kashif *m*

Kasimir

(Arabic); meaning 'explorer'.

Kasimir *m*
(Polish); meaning 'peace'.

Kaspar *see* **Jasper.**

Katharine *f*
(Greek); meaning 'pure'; other forms are Katherine, Catharine, Catherine and Kathryn and the short forms are Kath, Kathie, Kathy, Kate, Kitty and Cathy. Katie is in the top twenty of popular names for girls.

Kathleen *f*
The Irish form of Katharine; other forms are Cathleen and Caitlin.

Katinka *f*
A Russian form of Katherine.

Katrina *see* **Catriona.**

Kay *m*
(Gaelic); meaning 'a giant'.

Kay *f*
This name was originally a short form of names beginning with K. It has been used as a separate name for a long time; another form is Kaye.

Kayla *f*
This is a modern name which is popular in America; other forms are Kayleigh, Kayley and Kaylee.

Kedar *m*
(Arabic); meaning 'strong'.

Keefe *m*
(Irish); meaning 'noble'.

Keegan *m*
(Irish); meaning son of Egan; a surname used as a first name.

Keenan *m*
(Irish); a surname used as a first name.

Keir *m*
A surname used as a first name.

Keisha *f*
A modern name popular in America.

Keith *m*
A place name and surname used as a first name; this is a Scottish name which is now used worldwide.

Kelly *m* and *f*
(Irish); a surname used as a first name; another form is Kelley.

Kelsey *m* and *f*
(Old English); meaning 'victory at sea'; this is a surname used as a first name.

Kelvin *m*
(Gaelic); meaning 'narrow water'; the name of a Scottish river used as a first name.

Kendall *m* and *f*
A surname used as a first name.

Kendra *f*
The feminine form of Kendrick.

Kendrick *m*
(Welsh); a surname used as a first name; another form is Kenrick and the short form is Ken.

Kenelm *m*

(Old English); meaning helmet.

Kennedy *m*
A surname used as a first name.

Kenneth *m*
(Gaelic); meaning 'handsome'; the short forms are Ken and
Kenny.

Kent *m*
A surname from the English county which is used as a first
name.

Kentigern *see* Mungo.

Kenton *m*
A surname used as a first name.

Kenward *m*
(Old English); meaning 'brave guard'.

Kenyon *m*
(Welsh); a surname used as a first name.

Keren *f*
This is a short form of Kerenhappuch, one of the daughters
of Job; other forms are Kerena and Keryn.

Kerensa *f*
(Cornish); meaning 'love'; another form is Kerenza.

Kermit *m*
(Irish); meaning son of Dairmid.

Kerr *m*
A surname used as a first name.

Kerry *m* and *f*
The Irish county name used as a first name; probably first
used in Australia.

Kester *see* **Christopher.**

Ketan *m*
(Sanskrit); meaning 'home'.

Keturah *f*
(Hebrew); meaning 'fragrance'.

Kevin *m*
(Irish); meaning 'handsome'; the short form is Kev.

Keziah *f*
(Hebrew); meaning 'cassia', a spice; another form is Kezia.

Khadija *f*
(Arabic); meaning 'early-born child'; other forms are Khadeeja and Khadijah.

Kiara *f*
A modern name popular in America.

Kiera *f*
Another form of the Irish name Ciaran which means 'dark-haired'; other forms are Ciara and Kiara.

Kieran *m*
(Irish); meaning 'dark-haired'; other forms are Kieron and Cieran.

Kim *m* and *f*
(Old English); meaning 'royal'; another form is Kym.

Kimberley *f*
A surname used as a first name.

King *m*
A surname used as a first name.

Kingsley *m*
A surname used as a first name.

Kingston *m*
A place name and surname used as a first name.

Kiran *m*
(Sanskrit); meaning 'ray of light'.

Kirk *m*
(Old Norse); meaning 'a church'; a surname used as a first name.

Kirkwood *m*
A surname used as a first name.

Kirsty *f*
A Scottish short form of Christina; the Scandinavian version is Kirsten.

Kit *m*
A short form of Christopher.

Kitty *see* **Katharine.**

Klara *f*
The German form of Clara.

Klaus *m*
Another form of Claus.

Knight *m*
A surname used as a first name.

Knut *m*
Another form of Canute.

Konrad *m*
A German form of Conrad.

Kora *f*
Another form of Cora.

Krishna *m*
(Sanskrit); meaning 'black'; other forms are Krishan, Kishen and Kishan.

Kumar *m*
(Sanskrit); meaning 'prince'.

Kumari *f*
(Sanskrit); meaning 'a girl'.

Kurt *see* **Conrad.**

Kushal *m*
(Sanskrit); meaning 'intelligent'.

Kyle *m*
(Gaelic); meaning 'a narrow piece of land'; a place name and surname used as a first name; another *f* form is Kyla.

Kylie *f*
A modern name which comes from Australia.

L

Lacey *m* and *f*
A surname used as a first name.

Lachlan *m*
(Gaelic); possibly meaning 'warlike'; the short form is Lachie or Lochie.

Laetitia *f*
(Latin); meaning 'gladness'; other forms are Letitia and Lettice.

Laila *f*
Another form of Leila.

Laing *m*
A surname used as a first name.

Laird *m*
A Scottish surname used as a first name.

Lakeisha *f*
Another form of Keisha.

Lakshmi *f*
(Sanskrit); meaning 'birthmark'.

Lalage *f*
(Latin); meaning 'a babble'; short forms are Lal and Lally.

Lalita *f*
(Sanskrit); meaning 'charming'.

Lambert *m*
(Old German); meaning 'bright land'.

Lamond *m*
A Scottish surname used as a first name; another form is Lamont.

Lana *f*
Another form of Alana.

Lancelot *m*
(Old French); possibly meaning 'a servant'; another form is Launcelot and the short form is Lance.

Lane *m*
A surname used as a first name.

Lang *m*
A surname used as a first name.

Langford *m*
A surname used as a first name.

Langley *m*
A surname used as a first name.

Lara *f*
A short form of Larissa.

Lark *f*
The name of a bird used as a first name.

Larry *m*
A short form of Laurence.

Lars *m*
A Scandinavian form of Laurence.

Lascelles *m*
A surname used as a first name.

Latasha *f*
A modern name used in America; another form is Latisha.

Latham *m*
A surname used as a first name.

Latimer *m*
A surname used as a first name.

Laura *f*
(Latin); meaning 'laurel'; other forms are Lauren and
Laurencia and the short forms are Lora, Lori, Laurissa and
Loretta. Both Laura and Lauren are in the top ten of popular
names for girls.

Laurel *f*
The name of the tree used as a first name.

Laurence *m*
(Latin); meaning 'a man from Laurentium', a town in Italy;
another form is Lawrence and the short forms are Larry,
Laurie and Lawrie; the Dutch form is Laurens and the French
is Laurent.

Lavender *f*
The name of the plant used as a first name.

Lavinia *f*
The name of the wife of Aeneas; the meaning is uncertain;
another form is Lavina.

Lawson *m*
A surname used as a first name.

Lawton *m*
A surname used as a first name.

Lazarus *m*
(Greek); meaning 'helped by God'.

Leah *f*
(Hebrew); meaning 'cow'; the short forms are Lee, Lea and Lia.

Leal *m*
A surname used as a first name; another form is Leale.

Leanne *f*
Another form of Lianne.

Lee *m* and *f*
(Old English); meaning 'a meadow'; a surname used as a first name; another forms are Leigh and Lea.

Leena *f*
(Sanskrit); meaning 'dedicated'.

Leighton *m*
A surname used as a first name; another form is Layton.

Leila *f*
(Persian); meaning 'night'; other forms are Leilah and Laila.

Leith *m*
A Scottish place name used as a first name.

Lemuel *m*
(Hebrew); meaning 'devoted to God'; a short form is Lem.

Len *see* **Leonard.**

Lena *f*
A short form of Helen which is also used as a separate name.

Lennie *see* **Leonard.**

Lennox *m*
A place name and surname used as a first name.

Leo *m*

(Latin); meaning 'lion'; the French form is Leon.

Leonard *m*
(Old German); meaning 'bold as a lion'; the short forms are Len, Lennie and Lenny; another form is Lennard.

Leonie *f*
(Latin); meaning 'a lion'; the feminine form of Leo; other forms are Lea, Leola and Leona.

Leonora *f*
This is an Italian form of Eleanor; other European forms are Lenore and Leonore; the short form is Nora.

Leontine *f*
A feminine form of Leo; another form is Leontina.

Leopold *m*
(Old German); meaning 'brave people'.

Leroy *m*
(Old French); meaning 'the king'; popular in America; short forms are Roy and Lee.

Lesley *f*
A surname used as a first name; another form is Leslie.

Leslie *m*
A surname used as a first name.

Lester *m*
A surname, derived from the city of Leicester, used as a first name.

Levi *m*
(Hebrew); meaning 'attached'.

Lewis *m*
(Old German); meaning 'brave warrior'; another form is Louis

and the short forms are Lou, Louie, Lew and Lewie.

Lex *m*
A short form of Alexander.

Lexie *f*
A short form of Alexandra; also Lexy.

Leyland *m*
A surname used as a first name; another form is Leland.

Liam *m*
The Irish form of William. In the top twenty popular boys' names.

Lianne *f*
A short form of Juliana which is now used as a separate name; other forms are Leanne and Liane.

Libby *f*
A short form of Elizabeth.

Liese *f*
A short form of Elisabeth used as a separate name.

Lila *f*
A short form of Delilah.

Lilac *f*
The name of the plant used as a first name.

Lilian *f*
Originally a short form of Elizabeth, this is a separate name which is also related to the flower name Lily, meaning 'purity' with a short form of Lil; other forms of Lilian are Lillian, Lillah, Lila and Lillias.

Lilibet *f*
A short form of Elizabeth.

Lilith *f*
(Babylonian); meaning 'the goddess of storms'.

Lina *f*
A short form of Caroline.

Lincoln *m*
A place name and surname used as a first name.

Linda *f*
This is a German name which may have also been influenced by the Spanish word linda, meaning 'pretty'; other forms are Lynda and Lindy and the short forms are Lin and Lyn; Linda is also a short form of Belinda.

Lindell *m*
A surname used as a first name; another form is Lindall.

Lindley *m*
A surname used as a first name; another form is Linley.

Lindsay *m and f*
A Scottish surname used as a first name; other forms are Lindsey, Linsay, Linsey and Linzi.

Lindy *see* **Linda.**

Linet *see* **Lynette.**

Linford *m*
A surname used as a first name.

Linn *see* **Lyn.**

Linton *m*
A surname used as a first name.

Lionel *m*
(Old French); a French form of Leon meaning 'young lion'.

Lisa *f*
A short form of Elizabeth which is now used as a separate name.

Lisle *m*
(Old French); a surname meaning 'an island' used as a first name.

Lissa *f*
A short form of Larissa and Melissa.

Lister *m*
A surname used as a first name.

Litton *m*
A surname used as a first name.

Livia *f*
Another form of Olivia.

Lizzie *f*
A short form of Elizabeth; also Lizzy.

Llewellyn *m*
(Welsh); the meaning is uncertain but could be 'lion'; another form is Llywelyn.

Lloyd *m*
(Welsh); meaning 'grey'; another form is Floyd.

Locke *m*
A surname used as a first name.

Logan *m*
(Gaelic); meaning 'little hollow'; a surname used as a first name.

Lois *f*
This is a biblical name, probably Greek, the meaning of

which is uncertain.

Lola *f*
This name is a short form of Dolores and of Carlotta now used as a separate name; another form is Lolita.

Lombard *m*
A surname used as a first name.

Loretta *see* Laura.

Lorna *f*
A name invented by RD Blackmore for the heroine of Lorna Doone.

Lorne *m*
A Scottish place name used as a first name; another form is Lorn.

Lorraine *f*
This is the name of the region in France used as a first name; other forms are Loraine, Laraine and Lauraine and the short form is Lori.

Lottie *f*
A short form of Charlotte; also Lotty.

Louella *f*
A name formed by the combination of Louise and Ella.

Louis *see* Lewis.

Louise *f*
The French feminine form of Louis; another form is Louisa and the short forms are Lou, Louie and Lulu.

Loveday *f*
This name dates back to the Middle Ages and is still used in Cornwall.

Lovell *m*
A surname used as a first name; other forms are Lovel and Lowell.

Lowena *f*
(Cornish); meaning 'happiness'; another form is Lowenna.

Luc *m*
The French form of Luke.

Lucan *m*
A place name and surname used as a first name.

Lucas *see* Luke.

Lucasta *f*
A name created by the poet Lovelace.

Lucian *m*
(Latin); the meaning is uncertain; the French form is Lucien.

Lucille *f*
(Latin); meaning 'light'; this is the French form and the Latin form is Lucilla.

Lucina *see* **Lucy.**

Lucinda *f*
A poetic form of Lucy which is used as a separate name; the short forms are Cindy, Cindi and Cindie.

Lucretia *f*
A Roman family name used as a first name; another form is Lucrece.

Lucy *f*
(Latin); meaning 'light'; the Latin forms are Lucia and Lucina; other forms are Lucinda, Lucette and Lulu. In the top twenty popular girls' names.

Ludovic _m_
A form of Lewis; the short form is Ludo.

Ludwig _m_
The German form of Lewis.

Luella _f_
Another form of Louella.

Luigi _m_
The Italian form of Lewis.

Luis _m_
The Spanish form of Lewis.

Luke _m_
(Greek); meaning 'a man from Lucania'; another form is Lucas. In the top twenty popular boys' names.

Lundy _m_
A place name used as a first name.

Luther _m_
(Old German); meaning 'warrior of the people'.

Lydia _f_
(Greek); meaning 'a woman from Lydia' in Asia Minor.

Lyle _m_
Another form of Lisle; also Lyall.

Lyndon _m_
A surname used as a first name; another form is Lynden.

Lyn _f_
A short form of other names such as Linda, Lynette and Carolyn; other forms are Lin, Linne, Lynn and Lynne.

Lynda _f_
Another form of Linda.

Lynette *f*

This comes from the Welsh name Eluned meaning 'idol'; other forms are Linet, Linnet and Lynnette; the short form is Lyn.

Lynn *m*

A surname used as a first name; another form is Lyn.

Lysander *m*

(Greek); meaning 'a liberator'.

Lysandra *f*

The feminine form of Lysander.

Lytton *m*

A surname used as a first name.

Mabel *f*
A short form of Amabel which is used as a separate name; other forms are Mabella, May, Maybelle and Maybelline.

Madeline *f*
(Hebrew); meaning 'woman from Magdala', a town on the Sea of Galilee; the original form is Magdalene; other forms are Madeleine and Magdalen; the short forms are Madge, Maddy and Magda.

Madison *m* and *f*
A surname used as a first name.

Madoc *m*
(Welsh); meaning 'fortunate'.

Madonna *f*
(Italian); meaning 'my lady'.

Mae *f*
Another form of May.

Maegan *see* **Margaret.**

Maeve *f*
(Irish); meaning 'intoxicating'; this is a name from Irish legend; other forms are Mave, Meave and Meaveen.

Magda *f*
A German form of Magdalene.

Maggie *see* **Margaret.**

Magnolia *f*
The name of a tree used as a first name.

Magnus *m*
(Latin); meaning 'great'; the Irish form of the name is Manus.

Mahalah *f*
The Hebrew name of a city used as a first name.

Mahalia *f*
(Hebrew); meaning 'tenderness'.

Mair *f*
The Welsh form of Mary.

Mairi *f*
The Gaelic form of Mary; another form is Mhairi.

Maisie *see* **Margaret.**

Maitland *m*
A surname used as a first name.

Makepeace *m*
A surname used as a first name.

Malachi *m*
(Hebrew); meaning 'messenger of God'.

Malcolm *m*
(Gaelic); meaning 'disciple of Columba'; the short forms are Mal and Calum.

Malise *m*
(Gaelic); meaning 'servant of Jesus'.

Mallory *m* and *f*
A surname used as a first name.

Malone *m*
A surname used as a first name.

Malvina *f*
(Gaelic); meaning 'smooth brow'; another form is Melvina.

Manasseh *m*
(Hebrew); meaning 'bringing forgetfulness'.

Manda *f*
A short form of Amanda.

Manette *f*
A French form of Mary.

Manfred *m*
(Old German); meaning 'man of peace'; a short form is Manny.

Manish *m*
(Sanskrit); an Indian name meaning 'intelligence'.

Manisha *f*
An Indian name meaning 'clever'.

Manju *f*
(Sanskrit); meaning 'lovely'; related names are Manjubala and Manjulika.

Manley *m*
A surname used as a first name.

Manny *m*
A short form of Manfred, Emanuel and Immanuel.

Manon *f*
A French short form of Marie (Mary).

Manuel *m*
The Spanish form of Emanuel.

Manus *see* **Magnus.**

Marc *m*
The French form of Mark and Marcus; another form is Marcel.

Marcella *f*
The feminine form of Marcellus; other forms are Marcelle and Marcela.

Marcellus *m*
(Latin); the Latin form of Marcus and Mark.

Marcia *f*
The feminine form of Marcius, a Roman family name; other forms are Marcella, Marcelle and Marcelline and the short forms are Marsha and Marcy.

Marcus *m*
A Latin form of Mark.

Margaret *f*
(Greek); meaning 'a pearl'; this is a name with many forms such as Maisie (Scottish), Megan (Welsh), Mairead (Irish), Margot and Marguerite (French); other forms are Margarita, Margaretta and Margoletta and the short forms are Maggie, Madge, Meg, Greta, Meta and Rita.

Margery *f*
This was a short form of the French name Marguerite; Marjorie is the Scottish spelling and the short forms are Marge and Margie.

Maria *f*
This is the Latin form of Mary.

Marian *see* **Marion.**

Marie *f*

The French form of Mary.

Mariel *f*
A German short form of Mary.

Marigold *f*
The name of the flower used as a first name.

Marilyn *f*
A short form of Mary which is used as a separate name.

Marina *f*
(Latin); meaning 'from the sea'.

Marion *f*
A short form of the French name Marie which has long been a separate name; other forms are Marianne and Marianna.

Marius *m*
(Latin); derived from Mars, the god of war; the Italian form is Mario.

Mark *m*
(Latin); possibly derived from the name of Mars, the god of war; other forms are Marcus, Marc and Marcel.

Marland *m*
A surname used as a first name.

Marlene *f*
A German short form of Mary Magdalene; another form is Marlena and a short form is Marlee.

Marlon *m*
A name of unknown meaning.

Marlow *m*
A place name and surname used as a first name; another form is Marlowe.

Marmaduke *m*
(Irish); meaning 'servant of Madoc'; the short form is Duke.

Marsden *m*
A surname used as a first name.

Marsh *m*
A surname used as a first name.

Marshall *m*
A surname used as a first name.

Marston *m*
A surname used as a first name.

Martha *f*
(Aramaic); meaning 'a lady'; other forms are Marta and Martella and the short form is Martie.

Martin *m*
(Latin); meaning 'warlike'; the Welsh form is Martyn and the short form is Marty.

Martina *f*
The feminine form of Martin; other forms are Martita, Martinella and Martine; the short forms are Marty and Marti.

Marvin *see* **Mervin.**

Marwood *m*
A surname used as a first name.

Mary *f*
(Hebrew); meaning 'desired child'; this is a name with many versions such as Miriam, Mariam, Maria, Marie (French), Mairi and Mhairi (Gaelic), Maire (Irish), Mair (Welsh); other forms are Marietta and Mariella and the short forms are Molly, Polly, Mimi, Mamie and May.

Maryann *f*
A combination of Mary and Ann.

Marylou *f*
A combination of Mary and Louise.

Mason *m*
A surname used as a first name.

Matheson *m*
A surname used as a first name; another form is Mathieson.

Matilda *f*
(Old German); meaning 'mighty in warfare', the short forms are Matty, Tilly and Tilda.

Matt *m*
A short form of Matthew.

Matthew *m*
(Hebrew); meaning 'gift of God'; short forms are Mat and Matt. In the top twenty popular boys' names.

Matthias *m*
The Greek form of Matthew; another form is Mathias.

Maud *f*
An old French form of Matilda; other forms are Maude and Maudie.

Maureen *f*
An Irish short form of Mary; other forms are Moreen and Moira.

Maurice *m*
(Latin); meaning 'a Moor'; the short forms are Morrie, Maurie and Mo.

Mave *see* **Maeve.**

Mavis *f*
The word for a song thrush used as a first name.

Maximilian *m*
(Latin); meaning 'the greatest'; another form is Maximilien and the short forms are Max and Maxie.

Maxine *f*
The feminine form of Max.

Maxwell *m*
A surname used as a first name; the short form is Max.

May *f*
A short form of Margaret and Mary which is now a separate name; other forms are Mae and Mai.

Maya *f*
(Sanskrit); meaning 'illusion'.

Maybelle *f*
A combination of May and Belle.

Mayer *m*
A surname used as a first name; other forms are Meyer and Myer.

Maynard *m*
A surname used as a first name.

Mayo *m*
(Irish); a place name used as a first name.

Meave *f*
Another form of Maeve.

Meera *f*
(Sanskrit); meaning 'godly woman'.

Meg *f*

A short form of Margaret.

Megan *f*
A Welsh short form of Meg and Margaret; other forms are Meghan and Maegan. Megan is in the top ten of popular names for girls.

Mehetabel *f*
(Aramaic); meaning 'God is taking action'.

Mehul *f*
(Sanskrit); meaning 'clouds'.

Melanie *f*
(Greek); meaning 'black'; other forms are Melony and Melany.

Melbourne *m*
A surname used as a first name.

Melchior *m*
(Hebrew); meaning 'king of light'; one of the three wise men who worshipped the baby Jesus in Bethlehem.

Melisande *f*
The French form of Millicent.

Melissa *f*
(Greek); meaning 'a bee'; another form is Melinda and the short forms are Mindy and Melita.

Melody *f*
The musical word used as a first name.

Melville *m*
A surname used as a first name.

Melvin *m*
The derivation of this name is uncertain; another form is Melvyn and the short form is Mel.

Mercedes *f*
(Spanish); from 'Our Lady of the Mercies'.

Mercer *m*
A surname used as a first name.

Mercy *f*
This word can be used as a first name.

Meredith *m* and *f*
(Welsh); meaning 'great leader'; another form is Meridith and
the short form is Merry.

Meriel *see* **Muriel.**

Merle *f*
(French); meaning 'blackbird'.

Merlin *m*
The name of a small falcon.

Merrill *m*
A surname used as a first name; other forms are Merryll and
Meryl.

Merry *f*
The adjective used as a first name.

Merton *m*
A surname used as a first name.

Mervyn *m*
(Welsh); meaning 'sea fort'; other forms are Mervin, Merfyn
and Marvin.

Meryl *f*
Another form of Meriel.

Mia *f*
A Scandinavian short form of Mary.

Micah *m*
(Hebrew); meaning 'who is like Jehovah?'.

Michael *m*
(Hebrew); meaning 'who is like God?'; the short forms are Mike, Mick and Micky.

Michaela *f*
The feminine form of Michael.

Michel *m*
The French form of Michael.

Michelle *f*
The French feminine form of Michael; another form is Michele.

Miguel *m*
The Portuguese and Spanish forms of Michael.

Mikhail *m*
The Russian form of Michael.

Milan *m*
An Indian name meaning 'union'.

Mildred *f*
(Old English); meaning 'gentle power'; the short form is Millie.

Miles *m*
(Old German); the meaning is uncertain but is possibly 'merciful'; other forms are Myles and Milo.

Milford *m*
A place name and surname used as a first name.

Milla *see* **Camilla.**

Miller *m*

Millicent

A surname used as a first name; another form is Milner.

Millicent *f*
(Old German); meaning 'strong worker'; the French forms were Melisenda, Melisande and Melisent; the short forms are Millie and Milly.

Milne *m*
A surname used as a first name.

Milton *m*
A surname used as a first name; this name is popular in America.

Milward *m*
A surname used as a first name.

Mima *f*
A short form of Jemima.

Mimi *f*
An Italian short form of Maria.

Minerva *f*
The name of a Roman goddess.

Minta *f*
A short form of Araminta.

Mirabel *f*
(Latin); meaning 'magnificent'; other forms are Mirabelle and Mirabella and the short form is Mira.

Miranda *f*
(Latin); meaning 'to be admired'; the short form is Mira.

Miriam *f*
This is the oldest form of Mary; other forms are Mariam and Mariame and the short form is Mitzi, which is also the short

form of Maria.

Mischa *m*
A short form of Mikhail.

Mitchell *m*
This is a form of Michael used as a surname and a first name; the short form is Mitch.

Mo *m*
The short form of Maurice.

Mo *f*
A short form of Maureen.

Modesty *f*
(Latin); meaning 'unassuming'.

Modred *m*
(Old English); meaning 'a counsellor'.

Mohammad *see* **Muhammad.**

Mohan *m*
(Sanskrit); meaning 'attractive'.

Mohana *f*
(Sanskrit); meaning 'attractive'.

Moira *f*
This is the English spelling of Maire, the Irish form of Mary; other forms are Moyra and Maura.

Molly *f*
A short form of Mary now used as a separate name; also Mollie.

Mona *f*
(Irish); meaning 'high-born'.

Monica *f*
The meaning of this name is unknown; other forms are
Monique (French) and Monika (Scandinavian); Mona can be
used as a short form.

Monroe *m*
A surname used as a first name; other forms are Monro,
Munro and Munroe.

Montague *m*
An aristocratic surname used as a first name; another form is
Montagu and the short form is Monty.

Montgomery *m*
A surname used as a first name; another form is
Montgomerie and the short form is Monty.

Morag *f*
(Gaelic); meaning 'great'.

Moray *see* **Murray.**

Moreen *see* **Maureen.**

Morgan *m*
(Welsh); meaning 'born of the sea'.

Morgana *f*
The feminine form of Morgan.

Morley *m*
A surname used as a first name.

Morna *f*
(Gaelic); meaning 'beloved'; another form is Myrna.

Morris *m*
Another form of Maurice; the short form is Mo.

Mortimer *m*

An aristocratic surname adopted as a first name; the short forms are Mort and Morty.

Morton *m*

A surname used as a first name.

Morven *f*

A Scottish place name used as a first name.

Morwenna *f*

The meaning of this Welsh name is uncertain; another form is Morwen.

Moses *m*

The meaning is uncertain and it is probably Egyptian, not Hebrew.

Muhammad *m*

The name of the prophet meaning 'praise'; other forms are Mohammad and Mohammed.

Muhsin *m*

(Arabic); meaning 'charitable'.

Muhsina *f*

(Arabic); meaning 'kind-hearted'.

Muir *m*

A surname used as a first name.

Muirne *f*

(Irish); meaning 'well-loved'.

Mungo *m*

(Gaelic); meaning 'beloved'; the name of the patron saint of Glasgow.

Munir *m*

(Arabic); meaning 'brilliant'; another form is Muneer.

Munira *f*
(Arabic); meaning 'brilliant'.

Murad *m*
(Arabic); meaning 'desired'.

Murali *f*
(Sanskrit); meaning 'a flute'.

Murdo *m*
(Gaelic); meaning 'seaman'; another form is Murdoch.

Muriel *f*
(Celtic); meaning 'bright sea'; other forms are Meriel, Meryl and Merrill.

Murray *m*
A surname used as a first name; another form is Moray.

Mustafa *m*
(Arabic); meaning 'chosen'.

Myer *m*
A surname used as a first name.

Myfanwy *f*
(Welsh); meaning 'my fine one'; the short forms are Fanny and Myfi.

Myles *see* **Miles.**

Myra *f*
A name invented in the 16th century by a poet, Lord Brooke; another form is Mira.

Myrna *f*
Another form of Morna.

Myron *m*
(Greek); meaning 'fragrant'.

Myrtle ƒ
The name of the flower used as a first name.

Nadezhda *f*
(Russian); meaning 'hope'.

Nadim *m*
(Arabic); meaning 'a friend'; another form is Nadeem.

Nadine *f*
A French form of Nadezhda; other forms are Nada and Nadia.

Nafisa *f*
(Arabic); meaning 'exquisite'; another form is Nafeesa.

Nahum *m*
(Hebrew); meaning 'consoler'.

Naim *m*
(Arabic); meaning 'contented'.

Naima *f*
(Arabic); meaning 'peaceful'; another form is Naeema.

Nan *f*
A short form of Ann.

Nancy *f*
This was a short form of Ann but has long been a separate name; another form is Nancie and French forms are Nana and Nanette.

Naomi *f*

Napier

(Hebrew); meaning 'pleasant'.

Napier *m*
A surname used as a first name.

Nash *m*
A surname used as a first name.

Nat *see* **Nathan** and **Nathaniel.**

Natalie *f*
(Latin); meaning 'the Lord's birthday', or Christmas; the name was used in Russia as Natalya and Natasha; another form is Natalia and the short form is Tasha.

Nathan *m*
(Hebrew); meaning 'a gift'; the short form is Nat.

Nathaniel *m*
(Hebrew); meaning 'given by God'; the short form is Nat.

Nayan *m*
(Sanskrit); meaning 'an eye'.

Nayana *f*
(Sanskrit); meaning 'lovely eyes'.

Neal *m*
(Irish); meaning 'a champion'; another form is Neale.

Ned *see* **Edward.**

Neha *f*
An Indian name meaning 'rain'.

Nehemiah *m*
(Hebrew); meaning 'consolation of Jehovah'.

Neil *m*
(Gaelic); meaning 'a champion'; other forms are Nial and

Niall.

Nell *f*
A short form of Ellen, Eleanor and Helen; another form is Nelly.

Nelson *m*
A surname used as a first name.

Nero *m*
(Latin); meaning 'black-haired'.

Nerys *f*
(Welsh); meaning 'a lady'.

Nessa *f*
A short form of Agnes and Vanessa; another form is Nessie.

Nesta *f*
A Welsh short form of Agnes.

Nestor *m*
(Greek); meaning 'homecoming'.

Netta *f*
A Scottish short form of Janet.

Neville *m*
A surname used as a first name; another form is Nevil.

Nevin *m*
A surname used as a first name.

Newland *m*
A surname used as a first name.

Newlyn *m*
A Cornish place name and surname used as a first name.

Newman *m*

A surname used as a first name.

Newton *m*
A surname used as a first name.

Niall *m*
(Gaelic); meaning 'a champion'; other forms are Nial and Neil.

Niamh *f*
(Irish); meaning 'brightness'.

Nicholas *m*
(Greek); meaning 'victory of the people'; other forms are Nick and Nicky.

Nicola *f*
The feminine form of Nicholas; other forms are Nicole and Nicoletta; the short forms are Nickie, Nikki and Nicci.

Nigel *m*
(Latin); meaning 'black'.

Nikhil *m*
(Sanskrit); meaning 'complete'.

Nikita *f*
An Indian name meaning 'earth'.

Niloufer *f*
An Indian name meaning 'heavenly being'; another form is Neelofar.

Nils *m*
A Scandinavian form of Neil.

Nina *f*
A Russian short form of Anne which is used as a separate name.

Ninette *f*
A French short form of Anne.

Ninian *m*
The name of a Scottish saint who brought Christianity to the south of Scotland.

Nisha *f*
An Indian name meaning 'night'.

Nishant *f*
An Indian name meaning 'dawn'.

Nita *f*
A Spanish short form of Juanita.

Nixon *m*
A surname used as a first name; another form is Nickson.

Noah *m*
(Hebrew); meaning 'long-lived'; this is a name which is becoming popular once more.

Noble *m*
A surname used as a first name.

Noel *m* and *f*
(Old French); derived from Latin referring to Christmas Day; another form is Noelle and Nowell.

Nola *f*
(Irish); meaning 'white-shouldered'; this is a short form of Finola.

Nolan *m*
A surname used as a first name.

Nona *f*
(Latin); meaning 'ninth'.

Nora *f*
A short form of Eleanor, Honora and Leonora now used as a separate name; the short forms are Nonie and Noreen.

Norma *f*
(Latin); possibly meaning 'rule'; it is also a feminine form of Norman.

Norman *m*
(Old English); meaning 'northman'; a Viking and then a French name; the short forms are Norm and Norrie.

Northcliffe *m*
A surname used as a first name.

Norton *m*
A surname used as a first name.

Norward *m*
A surname used as a first name.

Norwood *m*
A surname used as a first name.

Nuala *f*
A short form of Fionnuala.

Nye *see* **Aneurin.**

O

Oakley *m*
A surname used as a first name.

Obadiah *m*
(Hebrew); meaning 'serving Jehovah'.

Oberon *see* **Aubrey.**

Octavia *f*
(Latin); meaning 'eighth'; the feminine form of Octavius, derived from a Roman family name.

Octavius *m*
(Latin); meaning 'eighth'; a Roman family name used as a first name; another form is Octavian.

Odette *f*
A French form of Ottilie; another form is Odile.

Odo *m*
(Old English); meaning 'rich'.

Ogden *m*
A surname used as a first name.

Ogilvie *m*
A Scottish surname used as a first name; another form is Ogilvy.

Olaf *m*
(Old Norse); meaning 'his ancestors' heir'; another form is

Olga

Olav.

Olga *f*
The Russian form of Helga.

Oliver *m*
(Old French); meaning 'olive tree'; the short forms are Ol and Ollie.

Olivia *f*
(Latin); meaning 'olive'; the feminine form of Oliver; another form is Olive and the short form is Livia. Olivia is in the top twenty of popular names for girls.

Olwen *f*
(Welsh); meaning 'white trail'; another form is Olwyn.

Omar *m*
(Arabic); meaning 'flourishing'.

Oonagh *f*
Another form of the ancient Irish name Una; also Oona.

Opal *f*
The name of the gemstone used as a first name.

Ophelia *f*
(Greek); meaning 'succour'.

Ophrah *f*
(Hebrew); meaning 'a gazelle'; other forms are Ofra and Oprah.

Oriana *f*
(Latin); possibly meaning 'to rise'.

Oriel *f*
Another form of Aurelia; also Oriole.

Orion *m*

(Greek); meaning 'son of light'.

Orla *f*
(Irish); meaning 'golden princess'; other forms are Orlagh and Orlaith.

Orlanda *f*
The feminine form of Orlando.

Orlando *m*
This is the Italian form of Roland.

Ormond *m*
A surname used as a first name; another form is Ormonde.

Orson *m*
(Old French); meaning 'small bear'.

Orville *m*
This name is little used in Britain but does appear in America.

Osbert *m*
(Old English); meaning 'bright god'; the short forms are Oz and Ozzy.

Osborn *m*
(Old English); meaning 'a godlike man'.

Osborne *m*
A surname used as a first name; another form is Osbourne.

Oscar *m*
(Old English); meaning 'the spear of God'; another form found in America is Oskar.

Osman *m*
(Arabic); meaning 'a little bustard'.

Osmond *m*

Ossian

(Old English); meaning 'protected by God'; the short form is Ossie.

Ossian *m*
A name from legend meaning 'little deer'.

Oswald *m*
(Old English); meaning 'the power of God'; the short forms are Oz and Ozzy.

Oswin *m*
(Old English); meaning 'friend of God'.

Ottavia *f*
The Italian form of Octavia.

Ottilie *f*
(Old German); meaning 'wealth'; the old form is Ottilia and other forms are Ottoline and the French Odette and Odile.

Otis *m*
A surname used as a first name.

Otto *m*
(Old German); meaning 'wealthy'.

Owen *m*
(Welsh); meaning 'a lamb'; this is a very popular name in Wales; another form is Owain.

Oxford *m*
A place name used as a first name.

Oxton *m*
A surname used as a first name.

P

Pablo *m*
The Spanish form of Paul.

Paddy *m*
This is a short form of Patrick and is used as a nickname for an Irishman.

Padma *m* and *f*
(Sanskrit); meaning 'lotus'; other forms are Padmad, Padmal, Padmini, Padman and Padmavati.

Padraig *m*
The Irish form of Patrick.

Paget *m*
A surname used as a first name; other forms are Pagett, Padget and Padgett.

Paige *f*
A surname used as a first name.

Paloma *f*
(Spanish); meaning 'dove'.

Pamela *f*
(Greek); meaning 'honey'; the short form is Pam.

Pancho *m*
A short form of Francisco.

Pandora *f*

Pansy

(Greek); meaning 'clever'; a name from Greek mythology.

Pansy *f*
The name of the flower used as a first name.

Paola *f*
The Italian form of Paula.

Paolo *m*
The Italian form of Paul.

Parvati *f*
(Sanskrit); meaning 'from the mountain'.

Pascal *m*
(Middle English); meaning 'Easter'; the form used in Cornwall is Pascoe.

Pascale *f*
(French); meaning 'Easter'.

Patience *f*
The word for the virtue used as a first name.

Patricia *f*
(Latin); meaning 'high-born'; the feminine form of Patrick; the short forms are Pat, Patsy, Patti. Pattie, Patty and Tricia.

Patrick *m*
(Latin); meaning 'a nobleman'; Patrick is the patron saint of Ireland; the short forms are Pat and Paddy and the Irish form is Padraig.

Paul *m*
(Latin); meaning 'small'.

Paula *f*
The feminine form of Paul; other forms are Paulina, Pauline and Paulette and a short form is Polly.

Payal *f*
An Indian name meaning 'ankle decoration'.

Payne *m*
A surname used as a first name; another form is Payn.

Pearl *f*
The name of the gem used as a first name.

Pedro *m*
The Spanish and Portuguese form of Peter.

Peer *m*
A Scandinavian form of Peter; another form is Per.

Peg *f*
A short form of Margaret; other forms are Peggie and Peggy.

Penelope *f*
This name comes from Greek legend and Penelope was the faithful wife of Odysseus; the short forms are Pen and Penny.

Peony *f*
The name of a plant used as a first name.

Pepe *m*
A short form of Jose.

Perceval *m*
(Old French); meaning 'he who pierces the valley'; this name comes from old French literature; another form is Percival and the short forms are Perce, Percy or Val.

Percy *m*
A short form of Perceval and also a surname used as a first name.

Perdita *f*
(Latin); meaning 'lost'; a name created by Shakespeare for *A*

Winter's Tale.

Peregrine *m*
(Latin); meaning 'a pilgrim or traveller'; the short form is Perry.

Perry *m*
A short form of Peregrine and also a surname used as a first name.

Persephone *f*
In Greek mythology this was the name of the goddess of spring.

Persis *f*
(Greek); meaning 'a woman from Persia'.

Peter *m*
(Greek); meaning 'a stone'; this as a translation of the Aramaic Cephas, the name given to Simon by Jesus; the French form is Piers and the short form is Pete.

Petra *f*
The feminine form of Peter; other forms are Petrina and Peta.

Petronella *f*
Derived from a Roman family name and used as a first name; another form is Petronilla.

Petula *f*
(Latin); meaning 'a seeker'.

Petunia *f*
The name of the plant used as a first name.

Phelim *m*
The Irish form of Felix.

Phemie *see* **Euphemia.**

Philbert *m*

(Old German); meaning 'bright'; another form is Philibert.

Philemon *m*

(Greek); meaning 'a kiss'.

Philip *m*

(Greek); meaning 'lover of horses'; another form is Phillip and the short forms are Phil and Pip.

Philippa *f*

(Greek); meaning 'lover of horses'; the feminine form of Philip; other forms are Philipa and Phillippa and the short form is Pippa.

Philomena *f*

(Greek); meaning 'well-loved'.

Phineas *m*

(Egyptian); meaning 'the black man'.

Phoebe *f*

(Greek); meaning 'the moon'; another form is Phebe.

Phyllis *f*

(Greek); meaning 'leafy'; another form is Phyllida.

Pia *f*

(Latin); meaning 'pious'.

Pierce *m*

A surname used as a first name.

Pierre *m*

The French form of Peter.

Piers *m*

Another form of Peter.

Pierse *m*

Pius

A surname used as a first name.

Pius *m*
(Latin); meaning 'holy'.

Polly *f*
A short form of Mary which is used as a separate name.

Pollyanna *f*
A combination of Polly and Anna.

Pooja *f*
An Indian name meaning 'worship'; another form is Puja.

Poojan *m*
(Sanskrit); meaning 'worshipped'; another form is Pujan.

Poojita *f*
An Indian name meaning 'one who is worshipped'; another form is Pujita.

Poonam *f*
An Indian name meaning 'full moon'; another form is Punam.

Poppy *f*
The name of the flower used as a first name.

Portia *f*
A Roman family name used as a first name.

Pratik *m*
(Sanskrit); meaning 'symbol'.

Presley *m*
A surname used as a first name.

Primrose *f*
The name of the flower used as a first name.

Priscilla *f*

(Latin); meaning 'former'; the short forms are Cilla, Pris and Prissy.

Priya *m*
An Indian name meaning 'beloved'.

Priyal *f*
An Indian name meaning 'well-loved'; other forms are Priyam, Priyanka and Priyasha.

Prudence *f*
The name of the virtue used as a first name; the short forms are Prue, Pru and Prudie.

Prunella *f*
(Latin); meaning 'little plum'; the short forms are as for Prudence.

Primo *m*
(Latin); meaning 'the first born'.

Pugh *m*
A surname used as a first name.

Punit *m*
An Indian name meaning 'pure'.

Punita *f*
An Indian name meaning 'pure'.

Q

Qasim *m*
(Arabic); meaning 'one who gives food to the people'.

Queenie *f*
This is a nickname for Regina, Latin for Queen; it has been used as a separate name.

Quentin *m*
(Latin); meaning 'fifth'; another form is Quintin.

Querida *f*
(Spanish); meaning 'well-loved'.

Quigley *m*
A surname used as a first name; another form is Quigly.

Quincy *m*
A French place name used as a first name; another form is Quincey.

Quinn *m*
A surname used as a first name.

Quinta *f*
The feminine form of Quinto.

R

Rab *m*
A Scottish short form of Robert; another form is Rabbie.

Rabiah *f*
(Arabic); meaning 'garden'.

Rachel *f*
(Hebrew); meaning 'ewe'; the short forms are Rachie, Rae and Ray and other forms are Rachelle, Rochell and Raquel (Spanish).

Radcliffe *m*
A surname used as a first name.

Radha *f*
(Sanskrit); meaning 'fulfilment'; another form is Radhika.

Radhakrishna *m*
An Indian name which describes the complete God.

Rafferty *m*
A surname used as a first name.

Rahil *f*
An Arabic form of Rachel.

Rahim *m*
(Arabic); meaning 'merciful'; another form is Raheem.

Rahima *f*
(Arabic); meaning 'full of mercy'; another form is Raheema.

Rainier *m*
A French form of Rayner.

Raja *m*
(Arabic); meaning 'hope'.

Rajan *m*
(Sanskrit); meaning 'the king'; another form is Rajesh.

Rajani *f*
(Sanskrit); meaning 'the dark one'.

Rajni *f*
(Sanskrit); meaning 'the queen'.

Rajnish *m*
(Sanskrit); meaning 'the moon'; another form is Rajneesh.

Raleigh *m*
A surname used as a first name; other forms are Rayleigh and Rawley.

Ralph *m*
(Old Norse); meaning 'wolf counsellor'; other forms are Rafe and Ralf; the French form is Raoul.

Rama *m*
(Sanskrit); meaning 'pleasing'.

Ramon *m*
The Spanish form of Raymond.

Ramona *f*
The Spanish feminine form of Raymond.

Ramsey *m*
A surname used as a first name; another form is Ramsay.

Ranald *m*
Another form of Ronald.

Randal *m*
(Old English); meaning 'shield of the wolf'; the short form is
Rand and another form is Ranulf.

Randolph *m*
(Old English); meaning 'shield of the wolf'; this name is from
the same root as Randal; the short form is Randy.

Rankine *m*
A surname used as a first name; another form is Rankin.

Ransom *m*
A surname used as a first name.

Raoul *m*
The French form of Ralph.

Raphael *m*
(Hebrew); meaning 'God has healed'.

Raqib *m*
(Arabic); meaning 'a guardian'.

Rashad *m*
(Arabic); meaning 'maturity'.

Rastus *m*
A short form of Erasmus.

Raul *see* Ralph.

Raven *f*
The name of the bird used as a first name.

Ravi *m*
(Sanskrit); meaning 'the sun'; another form is Ravindra.

Rawley *m*
Another form of Raleigh.

Rawnsley *m*
A surname used as a first name.

Ray *f*
A short form of Rachel.

Raymond *m*
(Old German); meaning 'strong protection'; the short form is Ray.

Rayne *f*
A surname used as a first name; another form is Raine.

Rayner *m*
(Old German); meaning 'mighty people'; other forms are Rayne and Rainier.

Razina *f*
(Arabic); meaning 'fulfilled'.

Read *m*
A surname used as a first name; other forms are Reade, Reed and Reede.

Reading *m*
A place name and surname used as a first name; another form is Redding.

Rebecca *f*
(Hebrew); the meaning is uncertain; another form is Rebekah and the short form is Becky. In the top twenty of popular names for girls.

Redman *m*
A surname used as a first name; another form is Redmond.

Reece *see* Rhys.

Regan *m*

A surname used as a first name; other forms are Reagan and Rogan.

Regina *f*
(Latin); meaning 'queen'.

Reginald *m*
(Old English); meaning 'power'; the short forms are Reg, Reggie and Rex.

Reine *f*
The French form of Regina.

Remus *m*
(Latin); meaning 'an oar'; Remus was the brother of Romulus, the founder of Rome.

Renato *m*
The Italian and Spanish form of Reginald.

René *m*
(French); meaning 'born again'.

Renée *f*
(Latin); meaning 'reborn'; this is the French form; another form is Renata.

Renfrew *m*
A place name and surname used as a first name.

Renton *m*
A place name and surname used as a first name.

Reshma *f*
An Indian name meaning 'made of silk'.

Reuben *m*
(Hebrew); meaning 'behold a son'; the short form is Rube.

Rex *m*

(Latin); meaning 'king'; Rex is also a short form of Reginald.

Reynard *m*
(Old German); meaning 'strong and brave'.

Reynold *m*
(Old English); meaning 'might'.

Rhea *f*
In Roman mythology, the mother of Remus and Romulus.

Rhiain *f*
(Welsh); meaning 'a girl'.

Rhiannon *f*
(Welsh); meaning 'great queen'; other forms are Riannon and Rhianna.

Rhoda *f*
(Greek); meaning 'a rose'.

Rhodri *m*
(Welsh); meaning 'crowned leader'; this name comes from the same derivation as Roderick.

Rhona *f*
A short form of Rowena.

Rhys *m*
(Welsh); meaning 'temper'; another form is Reece.

Rian *see* Ryan.

Richard *m*
(Old English); meaning 'powerful ruler'; an earlier form is Ricard and the short forms are Dick, Dickie, Rich, Richie, Ricky and Rickie.

Richmond *m*
A surname used as a first name; the short forms are Rich and

Richey.

Rider *m*
A surname used as a first name.

Ridley *m*
A surname used as a first name.

Rigby *m*
A surname used as a first name.

Rigg *m*
A surname used as a first name.

Rina *f*
A short form of names ending in -ina.

Riordan *m*
A surname used as a first name; another form is Reardon.

Ripley *m*
A surname used as a first name.

Rishi *m*
An Indian name meaning 'wise man'.

Rita *f*
A short form of Margarita used as a separate name.

Roald *m*
(Old Norse); meaning 'famous leader'.

Robert *m*
(Old German); meaning 'bright fame'; the short forms are Bob, Bobbie, Bobby and Bert and in Scotland Rab and Rabbie.

Roberta *f*
The feminine form of Robert; the short form is Bobbie.

Robin *m*
A short form of Robert which is now used in its own right; another form is Robyn.

Robina *f*
The feminine form of Robin; another form is Robyn.

Robinson *m*
A surname used as a first name.

Rochelle *f*
(French); meaning 'little rock'.

Rochester *m*
A place name and surname used as a first name.

Rodden *m*
A surname used as a first name.

Roderica *f*
The feminine form of Roderick.

Roderick *m*
(Old German); meaning 'famous rule'; the short forms are Rod and Roddy.

Rodger *m*
Another form of Roger.

Rodney *m*
A surname used as a first name; derived from a place name in Somerset; the short forms are Rod and Roddy.

Rodrigo *m*
The Spanish form of Roderick.

Roger *m*
(Old English); meaning 'famous spearman'; another form is Rodger and the short form is Rodge.

Rohan *m*
(Sanskrit); meaning 'healing'.

Rohanna *f*
The feminine form of Rohan.

Roland *m*
(Old German); meaning 'the famous land'; other forms are
Rowland and Rolland and the short form is Roly.

Rolf *m*
(Old German); meaning 'famous wolf'; the name is related to
Ralph and the short form is Rollo.

Roma *f*
The name of the city used as a first name.

Romilly *m*
A surname used as a first name.

Romney *m*
A place name used as a first name.

Romy *f*
A short form of Rosemary.

Rona *f*
The name of a Scottish island used as a first name; another
form is Rhona.

Ronak *m*
(Sanskrit); meaning 'enrichment'.

Ronald *m*
The Scottish form of Reynald and Reginald; another form is
Ranald and the short forms are Ron and Ronnie.

Ronalda *f*
The feminine form of Ronald.

Ronan *m*
(Irish); meaning 'little seal'; a name used in Ireland and Scotland.

Rory *m*
(Irish and Gaelic); meaning 'red-haired'; other forms are Rorie, Ruari and Ruaridh.

Rosabel *f*
A combination of Rosa and Belle; other forms are Rosabelle and Rosabella.

Rosalie *f*
(Latin); the annual Roman ceremony of hanging garlands of roses on tombs.

Rosalind *f*
(Spanish); meaning 'pretty rose'; other forms are Rosaline, Rosalin, Rosalinda, Roslyn and Rosaleen.

Rosamund *f*
(Latin); meaning 'clean rose'; another form is Rosamond and the short form is Roz.

Roscoe *m*
A surname used as a first name.

Rose *f*
The name of the flower used as a first name; other forms are Rosetta, Rosabella, Rosa, Rosina and Rosita; the short form is Rosie; the Irish form is Roisin.

Roseanne *f*
A combination of Rose and Anne; other forms are Roseanna, Rosanna and Rosanne.

Rosemary *f*
The name of the plant used as a first name; another form is

Rosemarie and the short forms are Romy and Rosie.

Ross *m*
(Gaelic); the name of a Scottish clan used as a first name.

Rowan *m*
(Irish); meaning 'red-haired'.

Rowan *f*
(Irish); meaning 'red-haired'; another form is Rowanne.

Rowe *m*
A surname used as a first name.

Rowell *m*
A surname used as a first name.

Rowena *f*
(Old English); meaning 'famous friend'; another form is Rowina.

Rowland *m*
An alternative form of Roland.

Rowley *m*
A surname used as a first name.

Roxane *f*
(Persian); meaning 'dawn'; other forms are Roxanne and Roxana.

Roxburgh *m*
A place name and surname used as a first name.

Roy *m*
(Gaelic); meaning 'red'.

Royce *m*
A surname used as a first name.

Royle *m*
A surname used as a first name.

Royston *m*
A surname used as a first name.

Rube *m*
A short form of Reuben.

Ruby *f*
The name of the precious stone used as a first name.

Rudolf *m*
(Old German); meaning 'famous wolf'; another form is
Rudolph and the short forms are Rudy and Rudi.

Rudyard *m*
(Old English); meaning 'an enclosure'.

Rufus *m*
(Latin); meaning 'red-haired'.

Rupak *m*
(Sanskrit); meaning 'beautiful'; other forms are Rupesh,
Rupchand and Rupinder.

Rupert *m*
(Old German); meaning 'bright fame'; this name comes from
the same root as Robert.

Rurik *m*
Another form of Roderick.

Rupli *f*
(Sanskrit); meaning 'lovely'; other forms are Rupashi and
Rupashri.

Russell *m*
A surname used as a first name; the short form is Russ.

Ruth *f*

(Hebrew); the meaning is uncertain; the short form is Ruthie.

Rutherford *m*

A surname used as a first name.

Rutland *m*

A place name used as a first name.

Ryan *m*

An Irish surname used as a first name; another form is Rian. In the top twenty popular boys' names.

Ryland *m*

A surname used as a first name; another form is Rylan.

S

Sabah *f*
(Arabic); meaning 'morning'.

Sabin *m*
(Latin); meaning 'a Sabine man'.

Sabina *f*
(Latin); meaning 'a Sabine woman'; the French form is
Sabine.

Sabrina *f*
This is a very old name which was used in Britain before the
coming of the Romans.

Sacha *m* and *f*
A Russian short form of Alexander; another form is Sasha.

Sacheverell *m*
A surname used as a first name.

Sadie *f*
A short form of Sarah; other forms are Sal and Sally.

Saffron *f*
The name of the spice used as a first name.

Sagar *m*
An Indian name meaning 'great sea'; another form is Saagar.

Sahil *m*
An Indian name meaning 'guide'.

Sahila *f*
An Indian name meaning 'leader'.

Sajjad *m*
This name means 'one who worships God'; another form is Sajad.

Salah *m*
(Arabic); meaning 'goodness'.

Saliha *f*
(Arabic); meaning 'kindliness'.

Salima *f*
(Arabic); meaning 'protected'.

Sally *f*
A short form of Sarah now used as a separate name; the short form is Sal.

Salma *f*
(Arabic); meaning 'peaceful'.

Salman *m*
(Arabic); meaning 'untouched'.

Salome *f*
(Aramaic); meaning 'peace'.

Samantha *f*
Probably a feminine form of Samuel; the short forms are Sam and Sammy.

Samima *f*
(Arabic); meaning 'honest'; another form is Sameema.

Samir *m*
(Arabic); meaning 'one who entertains with his conversation'; another form is Sameer.

Samira *f*
(Arabic); meaning 'lively conversation'; another form is Sameera.

Samson *m*
(Hebrew); meaning 'child of the sun'.

Samuel *m*
(Hebrew); meaning 'the name of God'; the short forms are Sam and Sammy. In the top twenty popular boys' names.

Sana *f*
(Arabic); meaning 'splendour'; another form is Saniyya.

Sanchia *f*
(Latin); meaning 'holy'; this is a Spanish and Provençal name; another form is Sancha.

Sandip *f*
This Indian name means 'lovely'.

Sandra *f*
A short form of Alessandra used also as a separate name; the short forms are Sandie and Sandy.

Sandy *m*
A short form of Alexander.

Sanford *m*
A surname used as a first name.

Sanjay *m*
(Sanskrit); meaning 'victorious'.

Sapphire *f*
The name of the precious stone used as a first name.

Sarah *f*
(Hebrew); meaning 'a princess'; the short forms are Sadie, Sal

and Sally.

Sarika *f*
An Indian name meaning 'cuckoo'.

Saul *m*
(Hebrew); meaning 'asked for'.

Savannah *f*
The name of a city in Georgia, USA used as a first name.

Scarlett *f*
The name of the heroine in *Gone With The Wind*; another form is Scarlet.

Scott *m*
A Scottish surname used as a first name.

Seamas *m*
This is the Irish form of James; another form is Seamus.

Sean *m*
This is the Irish form of John; other forms are Shaun, Shawn and Shane.

Searle *m*
A surname used as a first name.

Seaton *m*
A place name and surname used as a first name; another form is Seton.

Sebastian *m*
(Latin); meaning 'a man from Sebastia'; the short forms are Seb and Sebbie.

Secundus *m*
(Latin); meaning 'second'.

Seeley *m*

A surname used as a first name; another form is Sealey.

Sejal *f*
An Indian name meaning 'a stream'.

Selby *m*
A place name and surname used as a first name.

Selina *f*
The origins of this name are unknown although it could be derived from the name of the Greek goddess of the moon; another form is Selena and the French forms Céline and Célina.

Selma *f*
A name originating in Scottish literature which became popular in Sweden.

Selwyn *m*
(Old English); meaning 'the home of a friend'.

Senior *m*
A surname used as a first name.

Septima *f*
The feminine form of Septimus.

Septimus *m*
(Latin); meaning 'seventh'.

Seraphina *f*
(Hebrew); meaning 'high-born'.

Serena *f*
(Latin); meaning 'calm and serene'.

Seth *m*
(Hebrew); meaning 'compensation'; this is a popular name in America.

Seumas *m*
A Gaelic form of James.

Sewell *m*
A surname used as a first name; other forms are Sewall and Sewald.

Sexton *m*
A surname used as a first name.

Sextus *m*
(Latin); meaning 'sixth'.

Seymour *m*
A surname used as a first name.

Shahid *m*
(Arabic); meaning 'a witness'.

Shahida *f*
(Arabic); meaning 'a witness'.

Shahin *m*
(Arabic); meaning 'a falcon'; an other form is Shaheen.

Shamina *f*
(Arabic); meaning 'perfume'.

Shane *see* **Sean.**

Shani *see* **Sian.**

Shanley *m*
A surname used as a first name.

Shannon *m* and *f*
The name of an Irish river and place name used as a first name.

Sharad *m*

An Indian name meaning 'autumn'.

Sharada *f*
An Indian name meaning 'autumn'; another form is
Sharadini.

Sharadchandra *m*
An Indian name meaning 'harvest moon'.

Sharif *m*
(Arabic); meaning 'honourable'.

Sharifa *f*
(Arabic); meaning 'distinguished'.

Sharlene *f*
Another form of Charlene.

Sharmaine *f*
Another form of Charmaine.

Sharon *f*
(Hebrew); a Biblical area of great beauty used as a first name;
the short form is Shari.

Shea *m*
A surname used as a first name.

Sheba *f*
A short form of Bathsheba.

Sheena *f*
(Gaelic); a phonetic version of Sine, meaning Jane; another
form is Shona.

Sheila *f*
(Irish); a phonetic version of Sile, meaning Celia; other forms
are Shelagh, Sheela and Shayla.

Shelby *f*

Sheldon

A place name and surname used as a first name.

Sheldon *m*
A surname used as a first name.

Shelley *f*
A surname used as a first name.

Sherbourne *m*
A surname used as a first name; another form is Sherborne.

Sheree *f*
Another form of Cherie.

Sheridan *m*
A surname used as a first name.

Sherlock *m*
(Old English); meaning 'fair-haired'.

Sherwin *m*
A surname used as a first name.

Sherwood *m*
A place name and surname used as a first name.

Sheryl *f*
Another form of Cheryl.

Shirley *f*
A place name and surname used as a first name.

Shona *see* **Sheena.**

Sian *f*
The Welsh form of Jane; other forms are Siani and Shani.

Sibyl *f*
(Latin); meaning 'a prophetess'; other forms are Sibylla and Sybil.

Sidney *m* and *f*
This is a surname which has been used as a first name for almost three hundred years; another form is Sydney and the short form is Sid.

Siegfried *m*
(Old German); meaning 'peace from victory'.

Sierra *f*
A Spanish word for a mountain range used as a first name.

Sigmund *m*
(Old German); meaning 'safety through victory'; the short form is Sig.

Sigrid *f*
(Old Norse); meaning 'victory'.

Silas *m*
(Latin); probably a shortened form of Silvanus, the god of trees.

Silvester *m*
(Latin); meaning 'from a wood'; another form is Sylvester.

Silvia *f*
(Latin); meaning 'from the wood'; another form is Sylvia and the short forms are Silvie and Sylvie.

Simeon *m*
(Hebrew); meaning 'hearkening'.

Simon *m*
This is the English form of Simeon; the short form is Sim.

Simone *f*
The feminine form of Simon; the short form is Sim.

Sinclair *m*

Sine

A surname used as a first name; another form is St.Clair.

Sine *f*

A Gaelic form of Jane which in the English form is Sheena.

Sinead *f*

An Irish form of Jane; another form is Siobhan.

Sion *see* **John.**

Sissy *see* **Cecilia.**

Sita *f*

(Sanskrit); meaning 'a furrow'; other forms are Seeta and Seetha.

Skelton *m*

A surname used as a first name.

Skipper *m*

A nickname sometimes used as a first name; the short form is Skip.

Skipton *m*

A place name and surname used as a first name.

Skye *m* and *f*

A Scottish island name used as a first name.

Slade *m*

A surname used as a first name.

Smith *m*

A surname used as a first name.

Sneha *f*

(Sanskrit); meaning 'friendly'; another form is Snehal.

Snehin *m*

(Sanskrit); meaning 'friendly'.

Snowdon *m*
A surname used as a first name; another form is Snowden.

Solomon *m*
(Hebrew); meaning 'man of peace'; the short forms are Sol and Solly.

Somerled *m*
(Old Norse); meaning 'Viking'.

Somerset *m*
A place name used as a first name.

Somerton *m*
A place name used as a first name.

Sonal *f*
An Indian name meaning 'golden'.

Sonia *f*
A Russian short form of Sophia; other forms are Sonya and Sonja.

Sophia *f*
(Greek); meaning 'wisdom'; other forms are Sophie and Sophy. In the top twenty of popular names for girls.

Sorley *m*
An English form of Somerled.

Spencer *m*
A surname used as a first name.

Spring *f*
The name of the season used as a first name.

Sri *f*
(Sanskrit); meaning 'beauty'; other forms are Shree, Shri and Sree.

Stacey *m*
A short form of Eustace which is now used as a separate name; another form is Stacy.

Stacey *f*
A short form of Anastasia now used as a separate name; another form is Stacy.

Stafford *m*
A surname used as a first name.

Standish *m*
A surname used as a first name.

Stanford *m*
A surname used as a first name.

Stanhope *m*
A surname used as a first name.

Stanislas *m*
(Slavonic); meaning 'camp of glory'.

Stanley *m*
A surname used as a first name; the short form is Stan.

Stanton *m*
A surname used as a first name.

Stella *f*
(Latin); meaning 'a star'.

Stephanie *f*
(Greek); meaning 'a crown'; the feminine form of Stephen; short forms are Steffi and Steffie.

Stephen *m*
(Greek); meaning 'a crown'; another form is Steven and the short forms are Steve and Stevie; in Wales the name is Steffan

and in Europe it is Stefan.

Sterling *m*
A surname used as a first name; another form is Stirling.

Stockley *m*
A surname used as a first name.

Stockton *m*
A surname used as a first name.

Stoddard *m*
A surname used as a first name; another form is Stoddart.

Stoke *m*
A place name and surname used as a first name.

Storm *m*
This word is sometimes used as a first name.

Stowe *m*
A surname used as a first name.

Strachan *m*
A surname used as a first name; another form is Strahan.

Stratford *m*
A place name used as a first name.

Stuart *m*
(Old English); meaning 'a steward'; this is a Royal Scottish name; another form is Stewart.

Suhayl *m*
(Arabic); the name for the star Canopus; another form is Suhail.

Sujan *m*
An Indian name meaning 'trustworthy'.

Sumner *m*
A surname used as a first name.

Sunil *m*
(Sanskrit); meaning 'dark blue'.

Sunila *f*
(Sanskrit); probably meaning 'sapphire'.

Sunita *f*
(Sanskrit); meaning 'righteous'; another form is Suniti.

Suraj *m*
An Indian name meaning 'the sun'.

Surinder *m*
An Indian name derived from Indra; the short form is Sunni.

Susan *f*
(Hebrew); from the word Shushannah meaning 'a lily'; other forms are Susanna, Susannah; the French forms are Suzanne and Suzette and the short forms are Sue, Susie and Suzy.

Sutherland *m*
A place name and surname used as a first name.

Sutton *m*
A place name and surname used as a first name.

Swithin *m*
(Old English); meaning 'strong'.

Sybil *f*
Another form of Sibyl.

Sylvia *f*
Another form of Silvia.

T

Tabitha *f*
(Aramaic); meaning 'a gazelle'; another form is Tabatha.

Tadhgh *m*
(Irish); meaning 'a poet'; other forms are Thaddeus and Teague.

Taffy *m*
The Welsh form of David.

Tahir *m*
(Arabic); meaning 'virtuous'.

Taggart *m*
A surname used as a first name.

Talbot *m*
A surname used as a first name.

Talia *f*
A short form of Natalie.

Talitha *f*
(Aramaic); meaning 'a girl'.

Tallulah *f*
A place name in Georgia, USA used as a first name.

Tam *m*
A Scottish short form of Thomas.

Tamara *f*
(Hebrew); meaning 'a palm tree'; this is a Russian form of
Tamar and the short form is Tammy.

Tammy *f*
A short form of Tamara and Tamsin used as a separate name.

Tamsin *f*
This is a Cornish form of Thomasina; other forms are
Tamsine, Tamzin and Tamzen; the short form is Tammy.

Tanisha *f*
(Hausa); meaning 'a girl born on Monday'.

Tansy *f*
The name of a flower used as a first name.

Tara *f*
A place name, important in Irish legend, used as a first name.

Tasnim *f*
(Arabic); meaning 'fountain of heaven'.

Tate *m*
A surname used as a first name; another form is Tait.

Tatiana *f*
The name of a martyr venerated in the Orthodox Church. It
has long been popular in Russia; the short forms are Tanya
and Tania.

Tatum *f*
A place name and surname used as a first name.

Taylor *m* and *f*
A surname used as a first name.

Ted *m*
A short form of Edward, Edmund and Theodore; also Teddie

and Teddy.

Tegan *f*
(Cornish); meaning 'decoration'; another form is Tiegan.

Tejal *f*
An Indian name meaning 'shining'.

Terence *m*
This name is derived from a Roman surname; other forms are
Terance, Terrance and Terrence; the short forms are Terry and
Tel.

Teresa *f*
This is an old name whose meaning is uncertain; the original
form is Theresa and the French form is Therese; the short
forms are Tess, Tessa and Tessie.

Terris *m*
A surname used as a first name.

Thane *m*
A surname used as a first name; another form is Thaine.

Thecla *f*
(Greek); meaning 'glory of God'; another form is Thekla.

Thelma *f*
This name appears to have been introduced in the 19th
century as a character in a novel.

Theo *f*
A short form of Theodora now used as a separate name.

Theobald *m*
(Old German); meaning 'bold people'; the short form is
Theo.

Theodora *f*

(Greek); meaning 'God's gift'; this is the feminine form of Theodore; another form is Theodosia and the short forms are Thea and Dora.

Theodore *m*
(Greek); meaning 'a gift from God'; the short forms are Theo, Ted, Teddie and Teddy.

Theodoric *m*
(Old German); meaning 'ruler of the people'; other forms are Terry and Thierry.

Theophania *f*
(Greek); meaning 'the expression of God'; the short form is Tiffany.

Theophila *f*
(Greek); meaning 'beloved of God'; this is the feminine form of Theophilus.

Theophilus *m*
(Greek); meaning 'beloved of God'.

Thirza *f*
(Hebrew); meaning 'recognition'.

Thomas *m*
(Aramaic); meaning 'twin'; the short forms are Tom and Tommy and in Scotland Tam and Tammy; in the top ten of popular boys' names.

Thomasina *f*
The feminine form of Thomas.

Thora *f*
(Old Norse); in Norse mythology Thor was the god of thunder.

Thorburn *m*

A surname used as a first name.

Thorndike *m*
A surname used as a first name; another form is Thorndyke.

Thorne *m*
A surname used as a first name.

Thorpe *m*
A surname used as a first name; another form is Thorp.

Thurstan *m*
(Danish); meaning 'the stone of Thor'.

Tibbie *f*
A Scottish short form of Isabel and Isabella.

Tibold *m*
The German form of Theobald.

Tierney *m*
A surname used as a first name; another form is Tiernan.

Tiffany *f*
A short form of Theophania which is now a separate name.

Tilly *f*
A short form of Matilda; another form is Tilda.

Timothea *f*
The feminine form of Timothy.

Timothy *m*
(Greek); meaning 'honour to God'; the short forms are Tim and Timmy.

Tina *f*
A short form of Christina and similar names which is now used as a separate name.

Tiree *f*
The name of a Scottish island used as a first name.

Titus *m*
(Latin); the meaning is unknown.

Tiziano *m*
An Italian form of a Roman name related to Titus.

Tobias *m*
(Hebrew); meaning 'God is good'; another form is Toby.

Todd *m*
A surname used as a first name.

Todhunter *m*
A surname used as a first name.

Tom *m*
A short form of Thomas.

Tony *m*
A short form of Anthony.

Tonya *see* **Antonia.**

Topaz *f*
The name of the gem used as a first name.

Torquil *m*
(Old Norse); meaning 'Thor's cauldron'.

Torr *m*
A surname used as a first name.

Tory *f*
A short form of Victoria. Another form is Tori.

Tottie *see* **Charlotte.**

Townsend *m*

A surname used as a first name.

Tracy *m*
This popular name is probably derived from a French place name.

Tracy *f*
A short form of Teresa which is used as a separate name; other forms are Tracie and Tracey.

Traherne *m*
A surname used as a first name.

Travers *m*
A surname used as a first name; another form is Travis.

Tremayne *m*
(Cornish); a surname used as a first name; another form is Tremaine.

Trent *m*
The name of a river as a first name.

Trevelyan *m*
(Cornish); a surname used as a first name.

Trevor *m*
Meaning 'a large homestead'; the Welsh form is Trefor and the short form is Trev.

Tricia *f*
A short form of Patricia; another form is Trisha.

Triss *f*
A short form of Beatrice.

Tristram *m*
The meaning is uncertain but may come from the French Triste (sad); other forms are Tristam and Tristan.

Trix *f*
A short form of Beatrice; another form is Trixie.

Troy *m*
A name derived from the ancient city besieged by the Greeks; it is popular in America and Australia.

Trudy *f*
A short form of Gertrude; other forms are Trudie and Trudi.

Truelove *m*
A surname used as a first name.

Truman *m*
A surname used as a first name; another form is Trueman.

Tudor *m*
The Welsh form of Theodore.

Tulasi *f*
(Sanskrit); meaning 'holy basil', the plant.

Tully *m*
A surname used as a first name.

Tulsi *m*
(Sanskrit); meaning 'sacred basil'.

Turlough *m*
The Irish form of Terence.

Turner *m*
A surname used as a first name.

Twyford *m*
A surname used as a first name.

Tybalt *m*
Another form of Theobald; the short form is Ty.

Tyler *m* and *f*
A surname used as a first name; the short form is Ty.

Tyrone *m*
An Irish place name and surname used as a first name.

Tyson *m*
A surname used as a first name.

U

Udall *m*
A surname used as a first name.

Ulmar *m*
(Old English); meaning 'a wolf'; another form is Ulmer.

Ulric *m*
(Old English); meaning 'wolf ruler'; another form is Ulrick.

Ulrica *f*
The English form of the German Ulrike.

Ulysses *m*
(Latin); this is the Latin name for the Greek hero Odysseus.

Umar *m*
(Arabic); meaning 'flourishing'; another form is Omar.

Una *f*
This is a very old Irish name the meaning of which is unknown; other forms are Oona, Oonagh and Juno.

Unity *f*
The name of the abstract virtue used as a first name.

Unwin *m*
A surname used as a first name.

Upton *m*
A surname used as a first name.

Urania *f*
(Greek); the name of the Muse of Astronomy.

Urban *m*
(Latin); meaning 'from a town'.

Uriah *m*
(Hebrew); meaning 'light of Jehovah'; the short form is Uri.

Urian *m*
(Welsh); possibly meaning 'born in a town'; another form is Urien.

Ursula *f*
(Latin); meaning 'small she-bear'.

Uthman *m*
(Arabic); meaning 'a little bustard'. (Latin); a Roman family name used as a first name.

V

Vail *m*
A surname used as a first name.

Val *m*
A short form of Valentine.

Valdemar *m*
Another form of Waldemar.

Valentine *m*
(Latin); meaning 'healthy and strong'; the short form is Val.

Valentine *f*
(Latin); meaning 'strong and healthy'; another form is Valentina and the short form is Val.

Valentino *m*
The Italian form of Valentine.

Valerian *m*
(Latin); a Roman family name used as a first name.

Valerie *f*
(Latin); the name of a Roman family used as a first name; the short form is Val.

Vance *m*
(Old English); meaning 'young'.

Vanda *see* **Wanda.**

Vanessa *f*
A name created in the early 18th century by the writer
Jonathan Swift.

Vanna *f*
Another form of Gianna.

Vaughan *m*
(Welsh); meaning 'little one'; another form is Vaughn.

Velma *f*
A modern name of unknown meaning.

Velvet *f*
The name of the soft cloth used as a first name.

Venetia *f*
The name of the Italian city used as a first name.

Vera *f*
(Russian); meaning 'faith'; it is sometimes used as a short
form of Veronica.

Vere *m*
A surname used as a first name.

Verena *f*
The name of a 3rd century martyr; the name may be from the
same derivation as Vera.

Vergil *see* **Virgil.**

Verity *f*
(Old English); meaning 'truth'.

Vernon *m*
A surname used as a first name.

Veronica *f*
(Latin); meaning 'a true image'; another form is Verona and

the French form is Veronique.

Vesta *f*
The name of the Roman goddess of fire.

Vi *f*
A short form of Viola and Violet.

Victor *m*
(Latin); meaning 'conqueror'; the short form is Vic.

Victoria *f*
(Latin); meaning 'victory'; the short forms are Vicky, Vickie, Tory, Tori, Vita and Viti and there is also the nickname Queenie.

Vida *f*
A short form of Davida, the feminine form of David.

Vidal *m*
(Latin); meaning 'of life'.

Vijay *m*
(Sanskrit); meaning 'victory'.

Vijaya *f*
(Sanskrit); meaning 'victory'.

Vikesh *m*
An Indian name meaning 'moon'.

Vincent *m*
(Latin); meaning 'conquering'; the short forms are Vince, Vinnie and Vinny.

Violet *f*
The name of the flower used as a first name; another form is Viola, which is the Latin name for Violet; the Italian form is Violetta.

Viral *m*
An Indian name meaning 'beyond value'.

Virgil *m*
The name of the Roman poet; another form is Vergil.

Virginia *f*
(Latin); the name of a Roman family used as a first name; the short forms are Ginny, Ginnie, Gini and Jinny.

Vishal *m*
An Indian name meaning 'vast'.

Vishala *f*
An Indian name meaning 'wide-eyed'; another form is Vishalakshi.

Vita *f*
A short form of Victoria.

Vivian *m*
(Latin); meaning 'vivacious'; other forms are Vivyan and Vyvyan and the short form is Viv.

Vivien *f*
(Latin); meaning 'full of life'; other forms are Vivyan, Vyvyan and the French Vivienne; the short form is Viv.

Wade *m*
A surname used as a first name.

Wainwright *m*
A surname used as a first name.

Wake *m*
A surname used as a first name.

Waldemar *m*
(Old German); meaning 'famous ruler'; another form is
Valdemar.

Waldo *m*
(Old German); meaning 'a king'.

Walker *m*
A surname used as a first name.

Wallace *m*
A Scottish surname used as a first name in honour of Sir
William Wallace, the Scottish patriot; another form is Wallis
and the short forms are Wal and Wally.

Walter *m*
(Old German); meaning 'army leader'; the short forms are
Walt, Watty and Wat.

Walther *m*
A German form of Walter.

Walton *m*
A surname used as a first name.

Wanda *f*
(Old German); meaning 'a stem'.

Waqar *m*
(Arabic); meaning 'dignity'.

Ward *m*
A surname used as a first name.

Warne *m*
A surname used as a first name.

Warner *m*
A surname used as a first name.

Warren *m*
A surname used as a first name.

Warwick *m*
A place name and surname used as a first name.

Washington *m*
A place name and surname used as a first name.

Wasim *m*
(Arabic); meaning 'attractive'.

Wasimah *f*
(Arabic); meaning 'pretty'.

Waverley *m*
A place name used as a first name.

Wayne *m*
A surname used as a first name.

Webb *m*

A surname used as a first name.

Wendel *m*
(Old German); meaning 'one of the Wend people'; another form is Wendell.

Wendy *f*
The name was created by James Barrie in *Peter Pan*.

Wentworth *m*
A surname used as a first name.

Wesley *m*
A surname used as a first name; first used in honour of the Methodist brothers John and Charles Wesley; the short form is Wes.

Whitaker *m*
A surname used as a first name; another form is Whittaker.

Whitman *m*
A surname used as a first name.

Whitney *m* and *f*
A surname used as a first name.

Wilbert *m*
(Old English); meaning 'high-born'.

Wilbur *m*
A name used almost exclusively in America.

Wilfred *m*
(Old English); meaning 'aspiring to peace'; another form is Wilfrid and the short form is Wilf.

Wilfreda *f*
The feminine form of Wilfred.

Wilhelmina *f*

The feminine form of Wilhelm; the short forms are Elma, Minna and Minnie.

Willard *m*
A surname used as a first name.

William *m*
(Old German); meaning 'strong helmet'; the short forms are Will, Willie, Bill and Billy and an Irish short form is Liam. In the top twenty popular boys' names.

Williamina *f*
The feminine form of William; the short form is Willa.

Willoughby *m*
A surname used as a first name.

Wilma *f*
(Old German); meaning 'wishing protection'; a short form of Wilhelmina now used as a separate name.

Wilmot *m*
A surname, derived from William, used as a first name.

Wilson *m*
A surname used as a first name.

Wilton *m*
A surname used as a first name.

Wim *m*
A short form of Wilhelm.

Windsor *m*
A place name and surname used as a first name.

Winifred *f*
This name is derived from the Welsh and anglicized; the short forms are Freda, Win and Winnie.

Winona *f*
A Sioux word meaning 'eldest daughter'.

Winslow *m*
A surname used as a first name.

Winston *m*
A place name and surname used as a first name; often used in honour of Sir Winston Churchill.

Winthrop *m*
A surname used as a first name.

Winton *m*
A surname used as a first name.

Wolf *m*
(Old English); meaning 'wolf'; another form is Wolfe.

Woodrow *m*
A surname used as a first name.

Woodward *m*
A surname used as a first name.

Worth *m*
A surname used as a first name.

Wyman *m*
A surname used as a first name.

Wyn *m*
(Welsh); meaning 'white'; another form is Wynn.

Wyndham *m*
A surname used as a first name; another form is Windham.

Wynn *m*
A surname used as a first name; another form is Wynne.

Wynne

Wynne *f*
A surname used as a first name.

X

Xanthe *f*
(Greek); meaning 'yellow'.

Xara *see* **Zara.**

Xavier *m*
A surname used as a first name.

Xaviera *f*
The feminine form of Xavier; other forms are Xavia, Zavia and Xaverine.

Xenia *f*
(Greek); meaning 'hospitality'; another form is Xena.

Xerxes *m*
(Persian); meaning 'royal'.

Y

Yale *m*
A surname used as a first name.

Yasmin *f*
The original Persian form of the flower Jasmine; other forms
are Yasmine and Yasmina.

Yehudi *m*
(Hebrew); meaning 'a jew'.

Yolanda *f*
(Greek); meaning 'violet'; another form is Viola; the French
form is Yolande.

Yorick *m*
Meaning unknown.

York *m*
A place name and surname used as a first name; another
form is Yorke.

Yseult *see* **Isolda.**

Yuri *m*
A Russian form of George.

Yves *m*
(Old French); meaning 'a yew tree'.

Yvonne *f*
(French); meaning 'yew tree'; the feminine form of Yves; the

Yvonne

short form is Yvette.

Z

Zacchaeus *m*

(Hebrew); meaning 'pure'.

Zachary *m*

(Hebrew); meaning 'God has remembered'; other forms are Zacharias and Zachariah and the short forms are Zak and Zack.

Zahid *m*

(Arabic); meaning 'temperant'.

Zakiya *f*

(Arabic); meaning 'chaste'; other forms are Zakiyah and Zakiyya.

Zandra *see* **Sandra.**

Zara *f*

(Arabic); meaning 'to bloom'; other forms are Zahra and Xara.

Zaynab *f*

(Arabic); the meaning is uncertain; another form is Zainab.

Zeb *m*

A short form of Zebulun and Zebedee.

Zedekiah *m*

(Hebrew); meaning 'the goodness of Jehovah'; the short form is Zed.

Zelda *f*
A short form of Griselda.

Zelma *f*
Another form of Selma.

Zenobia *f*
The name of a famous Queen of Palmyra which was used in Cornwall.

Zephaniah *m*
(Hebrew); meaning 'God has concealed'; the short form is Zeph.

Zillah *f*
(Hebrew); meaning 'shade'; a favourite name with gipsys.

Zita *f*
(Italian); meaning 'little girl'.

Zoë *f*
(Greek); meaning 'life'.

Zola *f*
A modern name which probably comes from the surname of Emile Zola.

Zuleika *f*
(Persian); meaning 'shining beauty'.

My Favourite Boys' Names

Name	Page no

My Favourite Girls' Names

Name	Page no